AMERICAN
Education
IN THE 21ST CENTURY

by
Dan H. Wishnietsky

Phi Delta Kappa Educational Foundation
Bloomington, Indiana U.S.A.

Cover design by
Victoria Voelker

Phi Delta Kappa Educational Foundation
408 North Union Street
Post Office Box 789
Bloomington, Indiana 47402-0789
U.S.A.

Printed in the United States of America

Library of Congress Catalog Card Number 00-101822
ISBN 0-87367-828-1
Copyright © 2001 by Dan H. Wishnietsky

Table of Contents

Introduction

The turn of any century is an exciting time, but the start of a new millennium is cause for both awe and reflection, perhaps even for anxiety about what the future holds. After all, it has been 10 centuries, or 40 generations, since the last millennium began. Even computers had to be reprogrammed to work in the year 2000, a year that once seemed so far away. There was anxiety about a "Y2K" bug that might stop them and shut down stock markets and water, gas, and electric utilities. But the doomsayers were mostly wrong, as they usually are.

One wonders, however, about the real significance of this seemingly mystical advent. How important is the date 2000 (or 2001, whichever you believe is the real start of the third millennium)? Is the first year of the 21st century metaphysically significant? Or is the hype just that, just some excitement surrounding a numerical transition of human making?

The designation of the year 2000 is based on the calendar devised under the sponsorship of Pope Gregory XIII in 1582 in order to correct the Julian calendar, which had been used in much of the West since the Roman Empire. Yet the Gregorian calendar most of us use is by no means infallible. At its core is the presumed birth of Jesus of Nazareth, called the Christ; but historians have long expressed uncertainty regarding the birth year of Jesus. Some historians suggest that the year 2000 actually occurred somewhere between 1993 and 1997, believing that Christ actually was born between 7 B.C. and 3 B.C (in Gregorian years). Of course, it was the Gregorian calendar that gave us the familiar B.C. (before Christ) and A.D. (Anno Domini, after Christ's birth). Politically correct sensitivities now often render these as B.C.E. (Before the Common Era) and C.E. (Common Era).

In spite of this vagary, the Gregorian calendar holds sway throughout the developed world. But it has not entirely displaced other calendars not based on the Christian faith. Other calendars use other historical events as their basis. The Islamic calendar, for example, renders 2000 as 1420-21 (a change of year coming on April 5), based on events in the life of the Islamic prophet Mohammed, specifically his migration from Mecca to Medina. Other examples include:

- Japanese Year 2660, which began on 1 January 2000
- Chinese Year 4237, which began on 6 February 2000
- Indian (Saka) Year 1922, which began on 22 March 2000
- Byzantine Year 7509, which began on 14 September 2000
- Jewish Year 5761, which began 29 September 2000

The reality is that the Gregorian calendar year 2000 is just a number. Granted, it is a number with religious significance for some people; but it has no cosmic, metaphysical meaning. However, this reality need not diminish the importance of other reasons that mark the turn of the century and the start of a new millennium as significant. The years 2000 and 2001 do have symbolic importance. We can use them to reflect on our past, to examine the benchmarks of our cultural, social, and scientific attainments and thereby to clarify our vision of the future and set the course ahead. With this purpose in mind, we can convert symbolism into action. We can create the future we envision by setting real goals and working toward them.

In this book I have attempted to examine American education at this symbolic moment, to look back in general terms at where we have been and to suggest, also in broad terms, where education might be headed in the 21st century, with some considerations we might make along the way. The topics on which I have focused include a brief survey of the education "scene" today, the notion of a global village and ramifications for a global curriculum, technology related to globalism, diversity and equity issues, ideological and political issues, economic matters, the health of students, and lifelong learning. I have tried to include enough specifics to make the thinking points meaningful without turning this book into a tome.

What does, or should, the future hold for American education? I cannot pretend to have answers, being neither soothsayer nor futurist (if there is a difference). But I believe in asking questions that are not simply rhetorical. They require real answers. Different readers likely will arrive at different answers, all of which may be "correct" given the circumstances of the answerer.

Chapter 1

The Scene

No one would deny that the American education "scene" today is multifaceted, beginning with the multitude of school types available to parents and their children. There are public schools and private schools of every stripe, nonsectarian schools and religious schools, charter schools, and home schools. Even these are broad categories in which great diversity can be found among individual institutions, the people who run them, and the students they serve.

While the United States Department of Education influences education policy, actual control of schools is vested closer to home — in states, municipalities, local school boards, and other entities. The federal government controls only a few types of schools, notably those operated by the Department of State and the Department of Defense. As a result, schools are as varied as their locations. Public education is not the same from state to state, nor from community to community within any state. Private education is even more varied.

For simplicity, throughout this book I will focus mainly on public schools. But I would be remiss not to spend some time in this scene-setting chapter examining private education.

Volumes have been written about the history of American public education. The belief that everyone is entitled to an education evolved with the nation itself. Horace Mann in the early 19th century articulated a belief that every child had a right to a *public* education. His notion of a "common school" was one that embraced this right for all, regardless of economic or social status. Mann believed that education could solve societal problems, such as poverty and crime, and that there was a strong relationship between education and freedom. The common school would be the great equalizer and would encourage the maintenance of a republican system of governance.[1] Many modern advocates of the public schools voice this same philosophy.

The establishment of common schools and attempts in the middle of the 19th century to improve the condition of children led to compulsory school attendance laws. For example, the Compulsory Attendance Act of 1852 in Massachusetts stated that all children between eight and 14 years of age must attend school at least 12 weeks a year, and six of the weeks must be consecutive. The law was revised in 1873 to increase required attendance to 20 weeks a year. The movement toward mandatory school attendance continued to strengthen, and by 1918 all states had compulsory attendance laws. Today every state requires minors to the age of at least 16 to attend school.

The Public Purse

Public education is "public" by virtue of the public purse. Tax funds support the public schools, and the use of those funds is governed by a public entity, such as an elected school board. This system of tax support for public schools was established in the 19th century, but not without controversy. For example, in Kalamazoo, Michigan, the town had used tax money to support the public high schools for 13 years without complaint; but in 1875 a group of citizens sued to challenge the practice. Students were not required to attend high school, the complainants reasoned, therefore there was no reason for taxes to be used to support secondary education. The defending school officials countered that many court cases prior to 1875 upheld the use of public funds for secondary schools and that the Michigan Territory Code of 1827 required townships to maintain schools. The matter of compulsory attendance was a secondary issue. The court found in favor of the defendants and helped to establish grounds for other communities to establish tax-supported schools at all levels.[2]

Today, in fact, tax support has been extended beyond the secondary level to some forms of postsecondary schooling, such as community colleges. A number of plans are afoot to further extend tax support beyond those schools strictly considered "public" — that is, to private nonsectarian and religious schools, principally through the use of vouchers for public funds. Such plans are never put forward by disinterested parties, nor are they ever without controversy. Whether they will go forward or how far they will go remains to be seen.

Most American schools are public, and most students in the United States attend a publicly supported school. But parents have the right to direct their children's education, and they may opt for a private school alternative. In 1922 the state of Oregon attempted to require all children between the ages of eight and 16 to attend public schools. Parents who resisted could be fined. The law was soon challenged and reached the Supreme Court in 1925. The Court ruled: "The fundamental theory of liberty upon which all governments of this Union repose excludes any general power of the state to standardize its children by forcing them to accept instruction from public teachers only. The child is not the mere creature of the state, those who nurture him and direct his destiny have the right, coupled with the high duty, to recognize and prepare him for additional obligations" (*Pierce* v. *Society of Sisters*, 268 U.S. 510, 1925). Today statutes in every state affirm a parent's right to choose between public and private education.

It sometimes is helpful to remember that the public schools we cherish today did not exist in the beginning, when the "right" to a public education was still in the making. Until the common school movement in the mid-19th century changed matters, most children were educated in private schools of one kind or another. Boys were most likely to be schooled in these early times; girls often were underserved, if taught at all. But exceptions did exist. A rarity, for example, was the Salem Academy, which opened in the Moravian settlement of Salem, North Carolina, in 1772 as a "school for little girls" at a time when most Southern girls received no formal education. The academy, incidentally, continues to flourish in modern-day Winston-Salem.[3] It is, and always has been, private, not public.

Another example of a private school that educated an underserved group was the Institute for Colored Youth. Established in 1837 by Richard Humphreys, a Quaker philanthropist from Philadelphia, the institute attempted to counteract the practice of limiting or prohibiting the education of blacks. The institute started out as a high school and began offering its first postsecondary degrees in the 1930s. Today it is known as Cheyney University in Cheyney, Pennsylvania.[4]

A number of the historically black colleges and universities in the United States, and some schools in public education systems, began as private schools for minority youth. Private schools today continue to reflect the diversity of American society. Serving approximately 15% of the student population, private schools include military academies, Montessori schools, schools for the handicapped, church-related schools, and independent private academies, schools, and colleges. Census figures indicate that families that send their children to private schools represent the whole spectrum of American society, and many advocates of private schools believe that inner-city private schools contribute to community stability by providing alternatives to often-beleaguered urban public schools.[5]

Governance of private schools varies. Some are part of private school systems that can range from local to national associations. Others are part of loosely formed associations, and still others are completely autonomous. Supporters of private schools believe the freedom that private schools enjoy in governance and curricula is what gives the schools their distinctive character and diversity. But private schools are not wholly exempt from public governance. For example, the Supreme Court ruled in 1972 that states have a responsibility for educating their citizens and may impose reasonable regulations on the control and duration of basic education

(406 U.S. 205, 213). Because of the state's interest in having informed and self-sufficient citizens able to participate in a democratic society, the courts have ruled that states may impose limited regulations on private schools. These regulations are found in five general areas: record keeping and reports; licensing, registration, or accreditation; health and safety; curriculum; and public funding.

All states require either maintenance of school records or periodic attendance reports to ensure that children are not violating compulsory attendance laws. In most states, private schools need only to comply with basic education requirements and health and safety standards to be "approved." Health and safety standards include certification of immunization, regular fire drills, drug- and alcohol-free zones, and adequate safety in laboratory classes. Curriculum standards generally are characterized by broad statements, such as "subjects usually taught in public schools" or simply a list of basic subjects — reading, writing, mathematics, history, and so on. Although public funding of private schools is restricted — and a subject of seemingly endless debate — private schools may participate in publicly sponsored social welfare programs.

Many private schools are church-related, which contributes to the substantial tension over what public services and money private schools may legitimately use. Church-state separation has been, and likely will remain so in the foreseeable future, a hotly debated concept. Many court cases have tried to determine where the limits will be located. The guide most often used by judges when deciding recent cases is the three-part test formed by the Supreme Court in *Lemon* v. *Kurtzman,* 403 U.S. 602 (1971). The Court stated that public funds may be used by private schools when 1) the funding statute has a secular legislative purpose, 2) the principal or primary effect of the funding does not advance or inhibit religion, and 3) the statute does not excessively entangle the state with religion. Most of the public funds received by private schools are used for transportation of students, student health needs, and secular textbooks. However, many court cases arise each year in which citizens question the use of public funds in some private education context.

The Charter School Movement

In the late 1980s groups of parents, local educators, school board members, and community leaders developed a model of public schooling that was intended to improve student learning by providing the same governance flexibility to public schools as could be found in private education. These schools became known as "charter" schools because each school was formed by a performance contract, or charter. The planned school would submit a charter to prospective parents, teachers, the local school board, and the state board of education, stating the goals that the school aimed to achieve, how the school was to operate, and the length of time the school had to achieve its stated goals. If approved, the charter became the document for determining how the school was governed, thus replacing state and local policies and regulations.

By the early 1990s several states had passed legislation to permit the formation of these types of public school. But the standards are by no means universal. The freedom granted to charter schools varies by state. In some, charter schools are released from all regulations except those that apply to safety, health, and equal protection. An example of a state that frees charter schools from most state regulation is Georgia. The state's Charter School Act enables educators to rethink and redesign the charter school virtually from the foundation up. This includes choosing the curriculum, instructional strategies, student placement and scheduling, deployment of faculty and staff, school governance, money allocation, and community involvement. Other states are more restrictive in their treatment of charter schools.

As of this writing, more than half of the states allow charter schools, and this number is expected to increase. The growth of the charter schools movement has drawn the interest of the United States Department of Education. In 1994 amendments to the Elementary and Secondary Education Act committed funds for charter school development and for a national study to evaluate their accomplishments. According to Department of Education documents, the study will address the areas of implementation, effects on students, and effects on public education. Implementation topics include comparing charter schools with other public schools, determining the demographics of students who attend charter schools, and assessing the variables that influence charter school development. The effects on students will be assessed by evaluating the achievement of students at various charter schools and comparing it to the achievement of their counterparts attending traditional public schools. A meaningful aspect of this evaluation — because charter schools vary widely from one another, as well as from other public schools — will be to determine the factors that positively influence student learning. Finally, the Department of Education will assess how charter schools affect local and state public education systems. Some critics, for example, have expressed concern that charter schools may simply skim off the "cream" of public school students — a charge often leveled at (and largely untrue of) private schools.

The increasing interest in charter schools also was illustrated in the 1998 federal budget. Congress provided for an increased emphasis on charter schools by addressing a number of issues related to Department of Education money for state-approved charter schools. For example, the budget bill required the Department of Education to give priority in awarding grants to states in which the performance of every charter school is reviewed at least once every five years. This requirement was designed to ensure that the schools fulfill the terms of their charters and that students meet achievement goals. Charter schools that cannot meet their goals should not continue to exist.[6]

Congress also suggested that if states have made progress in increasing the number of high-quality, accountable charter schools, then they should be rewarded. A compromise between the Democrats and the Republicans resulted in the bill clearly stating that any charter school receiving funds must be measured by the same state assessments as are other public schools. Finally, because the purpose of reform is to improve education and successful programs need to be publicized, the budget bill provided new authority for successful charter schools to serve as models, not just for other charter schools but for public schools generally.

Critics of charter schools observe that many charter schools are not successful and cease to exist after a short time. In their defense, supporters of charter schools respond that the closing of some charter schools demonstrates that the charter school movement is indeed accomplishing its goals. The purpose of a charter school is to be innovative and attempt new education strategies. If successful, the school will attract students and continue to grow. Some innovations, however, will disappoint; and charter schools using methods that are not successful in educating students should change or cease to exist. This is as it should be. In contrast, according to the charter school proponents, a problem with traditional public schools is that failed methods continue to be used for too long. In 1999 the Department of Education seemed to support this allegation when it suggested that public schools that fail to adequately educate their students should face a loss of federal funds.[7]

Home Schooling

Another education alternative is home schooling. Most home schooling involves a parent providing instruction and learning at home in a family setting with one or more students who are members of the same family and who are learning K-12 material. Some students are schooled at home for health or other reasons, with the teacher hired and supervised by the local public school system; but this is not home schooling in the usual sense.

Parents who decide to teach their own children at home often have strong philosophical or religious beliefs concerning education. The common view of home schooling as a conservative Christian movement is often mistaken. Many home schooling efforts are conducted on the basis of Rousseau-like views; they are liberal, child-centered schools. Other home schooling efforts are taken up because of religious concerns based on other religions than Christian. For example, Muslim families may choose to home school their children in some cases because they believe public schools may be hostile to their religious beliefs.

Every state permits home schooling in some form, and the requirements for home schools vary from state to state. Some states require the home school teacher to be certified by the state, while other states place few requirements on the instructor's qualifications. Regulations that are fairly consistent across the country for home schools require home school teachers to submit attendance records to the state or local school district and to administer standardized tests to their students.

Because many home school teachers are not trained as educators, they use an apprenticeship model of education. This includes using simulated or real-life learning situations based on individual and community interests and inviting community experts in certain subjects to present information to the students. Several companies provide curriculum packages for parents who home school; however, most parents design their own curriculum using materials from several publishers. Students in many home schools help plan the curriculum and suggest activities. Often such schooling becomes a social endeavor as home schooling parents within the community collaborate for special classes, field trips, and extracurricular programs.[8]

Proponents and opponents of various schooling enterprises have engaged in sharp debates. The radical view at one end of the spectrum is that a democratic society should be supported wholly by public schools. Private schools siphon off those students best able to learn and thus create a socioeconomic elite. The radical view at the other end of the spectrum avers that public schools have failed in the public charge and that students and parents would be better served through the diversity of private schools. They point out that many private schools do not have restrictive admission policies. And the fact that many tax-paying parents are willing to shoulder the additional financial burden of a private education points to a high concern for their children and education in general that well serves the nation.

When the issue turns on home schooling, the debate is particularly sharp. Many home-schoolers allege that the public schools are dangerous places that are academically weak and present students with a worldview that often conflicts with the values their parents teach. At home schooling conferences, the public schools often are derided as "government schools." Many home schooling parents disagree philosophically with the mainstream of American education.

Critics of the home schooling movement counter just as sharply that home schooling is not schooling at all, but indoctrination. Home schooling parents are viewed as incompetent to teach the curriculum, and home schooling's most severe critics accuse home-schoolers of child abuse because the home school isolates children from their peers and inhibits their social growth.[9]

Somewhere there is a middle ground. In fact, it is occupied by most educators, parents, and students, who do not view the various forms of public and private education as mutually exclusive. A large number of public school educators work part-time in private school enterprises; and it is not unusual for private school teachers to be hired either temporarily or permanently by public schools. Because charter schools, though private in character, are public schools, most charter school educators are state-certified and were part of the public school system prior to moving into the charter school. Even home schools are not isolated from public education. Public school teachers often are invited to provide expert assistance to the home schooling parent, and many students are home schooled for only a portion of their school career. For example, they may be taught at home during their elementary school years and then be placed in a public school when they reach their middle or high school years, often because the larger public school can offer a wider, more in-depth choice of classes.

In short, while there are vast differences among schools of all types, there also are many similarities. Regardless of the type of school, students are taught the fundamental subjects of reading, writing, mathematics, science, history, and geography. Often they use the same or similar textbooks, and there may be few real differences in curriculum. For example, mathematics taught in the various types of schools is almost identical and, in many cases, follows the standards developed by National Council of Teachers of Mathematics.

Conflicts and Controversy

Differences may occur in the methods of teaching among schools, both public and private; but public debate often exaggerates those differences. One example is the discussion about whether students should be taught to read by using phonics or whole language. Although this has become a major debate among the public schools, home schools, and some private schools, the reality of the classroom indicates that differences among the schools probably are overstated. Some public and private school instructors teach reading emphasizing the whole language approach while other teachers emphasize phonics. But when one observes a typical classroom, one usually sees that the teacher is not using any single method exclusively, but a combination of methods. This is as true of home-schoolers as of public school teachers.

The real differences between the various types of schools tend to arise from matters related to worldviews and values. A good example of worldview conflict is the tension that arises in science teaching over evolution versus Bible-based "creation science." Often, but not always, these issues are related to religious beliefs, as in this example. Parents tend to choose private education based on the school's philosophy, seeking an alignment of values and a compatible worldview, which they have not found in the public schools. Public schools, by their nature, cannot be narrowly aligned in this manner. But most public schools attempt to minimize conflicts by allowing parents and students to "opt out" of activities or assignments on the basis of moral, spiritual, or ethical concerns and to be provided with alternative school work.

Health education and civic education also produce areas of conflict. Public schools, for example, are likely to include in the health curriculum information about sexually transmitted diseases and their prevention, because many school children are sexually active and need accurate information in order to make informed decisions that affect their health and safety. Private schools and home-schoolers, particularly if their basis is a conservative religion, may oppose such teaching as immoral. Often they favor teaching an abstinence-only curriculum or complete avoidance of any form of sex education.

In a similar manner the schools and parents may favor civic education that promotes a worldview based on their interpretation of religious documents, such as condemning other religious views, racial groups, or other segments of society. Religious schools are an obvious example of this, but private schools also exist along narrow racial lines — all black, all white, and so on. For some parents, the growing diversity — and the valuing of diversity — in the public schools can be a reason for turning away from them. An example of increasing diversity is the growing acceptance of homosexuality. Increasing recognition of the civil rights of gay and lesbian citizens is as uncomfortable for some conservative parents today as recognition of black civil rights was for some white parents in the 1960s. Other societal issues fall into this same category of controversy: abortion, affirmative action, feminism, and so forth. Each or all may serve as reasons for some citizens to favor a more narrow private education over a more diverse public education.

Much controversy arises over the extent to which parents believe they are able to influence or control the education of their children. It can be argued that, at least in the 20th century, there was greater uniformity of worldview and a greater sense of cohesion in school purposes until about mid-century. Christian mores and traditions of patriotism dominated. Teachers, particularly at the elementary level, led students in morning prayers and a daily recitation of the Pledge of Allegiance. The Christian influence in the public square and over the public schools was forceful. But as American culture became more diverse — and previously existing diversity was better recognized — that dominance was called into question. The courts began to take a firmer stand on church-state separation, and the public schools began to shed this religious dominance. Patriotism, too, took a beating in the wake of the Vietnam War and the accompanying antiwar movement. Anyone examining school routines regarding patriotism in the period prior to World War II and the period following the Vietnam War will find vast differences.

Politics and Schools

There is an African proverb: "When the bull elephants fight, it is the grass that gets trampled." Often the public dialogue about schools is shaped more by politics than pedagogy. Educators themselves are largely disenfranchised in school governance, which more often is the province of noneducators: local school boards, state boards of education, and other legislative groups. Thus a debate over the purchase of computers, for example, may turn more on financial considerations or legal concerns — Should students have access to the Internet? — than on curricular substance or instructional needs. Ultimately, students can be the losers when politics takes the upper hand.

Politics also plays a key role in questions of teacher competence and teacher testing. Superficially the questions are educational. Certainly teachers should be competent. But who controls competence? Simply graduating from college with the appropriate training is not deemed sufficient, because (to oversimplify) that would leave control of teacher competence in the hands of higher education. Therefore, the state must *certify* teacher preparation by issuing a teaching license. Control thus goes to the state, which can determine whether a teacher, regardless of degree, has taken the necessary coursework. But politicians in some states have found this level of control too limited because it simply is a validation of what happens in higher education. In these states a mandated teacher exam is used as a way of ensuring that what the college or university says happened (that the student, by virtue of graduating, has proven competence) actually did happen. Such testing is a further way for states to assert political power over education and educators.

This assertion of political power by states diminishes the positive effect of professional organizations in education, which might otherwise establish their own professional standards, certification, and the like. In the eyes of many critics, this type of political "interference" also keeps education from becoming a "true profession," by which professionalism is equated with self-governance.

Some politicians also urge teacher testing as a "quick fix" for school ills. If teachers are judged by a written test to be incompetent, then they are candidates for removal and replacement. Most educators, on the contrary, see teacher tests as superficial and a poor basis for drastic judgments, such as a ruined career. Teachers who fail to "measure up," they would contend, can be remediated through additional training, peer mentoring, and other processes — measures that teachers take (and are expected to take) when dealing with students who fail to demonstrate competence in given areas of learning. This approach is not politically expedient, nor does it make the kind of headlines that are made when politicians criticize schools.

Most educators believe that politicians have made the public schools scapegoats for society's ills during the past 20 years when, in fact, the schools are as good as, if not better than, ever. This is not to say that schools cannot or should not improve. The schools are facing many challenges today that they did not face in the past, and improvement is needed to meet them.

Criticism of schools, while often exaggerated or ill-founded, has resulted in political actions to reform education. A prime example is the Goals 2000: Educate America Act, signed into law in 1994, which already has helped to establish content standards, student performance standards, and opportunity to learn standards. Goals 2000 places emphasis on community planning for restructuring schools to meet the needs of the 21st century. Items covered include education goals, student achievement, parent assistance, international education programs, safe schools, civics education, and education research. The act also provides more than rhetoric; grant money has been made available to fund innovative programs.

Position and Influence

Two types of power are the power of position and the power of influence. The power of position in the public education arena is with the politicians. They hold the position in legislatures, on school boards, and so on. Therefore teachers must use their power of influence on these officials to bring about sound education decisions. Teachers and teacher organizations are becoming savvier in this regard. Instead of waiting for state legislatures or school boards to direct teachers regarding content, teaching, and assessment, teacher organizations are developing, based on sound pedagogy, their own content, teaching, and assessment standards. Instead of the politician "guiding" teachers, teachers are guiding the public to understand how high-quality programs should be developed and implemented.

National education organizations are setting an agenda for the schools more aggressively today than in recent memory. The basics can be stated in a few sentences:

- Every student deserves to be enrolled in an excellent program of instruction.
- Students should be challenged to achieve at their highest ability for productive citizenship and employment.
- Students should be taught by qualified teachers who expect students to demonstrate a high level of achievement.
- The curriculum should be complete and coherent at every grade level.
- Teachers should employ a variety of instructional approaches and diverse strategies based on curriculum content and student need.
- Content should be placed in context, and the curriculum should demonstrate how the various disciplines are interrelated.
- Technology should be an integral part of the curriculum.
- Assessment should incorporate information from various sources, such as standardized tests, teacher-made tests, quizzes, observations, performance tasks, and projects.

Making goals such as these a reality is the challenge for today's educators. When observing the political and economic realities affecting American education, the facts seem to indicate that internal and external influences can conspire to separate educators, the general public, and politicians. For example, some Americans seem to doubt that educators are willing or able to solve their own problems. Others believe that public school educators have willfully concealed problems from the public to protect themselves from negative publicity or consequences, and so community-generated methods and solutions must be legislated and implemented. To counteract this perception, teachers and administrators, on the whole, are working hard to address the problems found in public schools, to delineate well-informed and effective policies, to implement reasonable solutions, and to promote the accomplishments of the schools without hiding their shortcomings.

The education "scene" today might be characterized by a sense of mistrust, but that perception reflects merely the negative. Trust, which once seemed to be a given in public education, needs to be rebuilt. That is certain. But education today, and individual educators, cannot be cast solely in a negative light. Optimism and hope are powerful emotions, particularly as they are being activated by forward-looking plans, new programs, and future-oriented policies and practices — all of which are being pursued with vigor.

Notes

1. Frederick M. Raubinger, *The Development of Secondary Education* (New York: Macmillan, 1969).
2. Robert Barger, "The Kalamazoo Case," *History of American Education Web Project.* www.ux1.eiu.edu/~cfrnb/kalamazo.html
3. Salem College. www.salem.edu/about/abtfrm.htm
4. Cheyney University. www.cheyney.edu/aboutcu.html
5. Department of Education, "Introduction," *Private Schools in the United States.* nces.ed.gov/pubs/ps/97459003.html
6. Department of Education, "The State of Charter Schools 2000," www.ed.gov/pubs/charter4thyear

7. Melinda K. Malico, "Charter School Success to be Measured." www.ed.gov/PressReleases/09-1995/charteva.html

8. Erik Nelson, "Home Schooling," *ERIC Digest*, no. 15 (1986) ERIC No. ED282348.

9. J. Van Galen and M.A. Pitman, eds., *Home Schooling: Political, Historical, and Pedagogical Perspectives* (New Jersey: Ablex, 1991).

Chapter 2

Thinking Global

The term *global village* has been so overused that it almost has lost its meaning. A reality of the 21st century is that the world, the "globe," has become a collection of linked entities. Economic and cultural connections among nations are becoming the rule, rather than the exception. The globe really has been "shrunk" to the size of a village, at least in the "virtual" sense.

Canadian educator and futurist Marshal McLuhan formulated the idea of a global village in the 1960s, a time when global war sometimes seemed more likely than global cooperation.[1] While problems and conflicts still exist throughout the world, transnational interactions abound and are positive signs of cooperation and coexistence. The watchword today is *globalization*, and the maxim "think global, act local" has real meaning, no less for education than for business and industry, government, and culture. The global economy that seems to drive globalization in other aspects of life touches all of us.

Immigration throughout the world has produced populations in many nations that are now more multi-ethnic and multicultural than they were in the past. This is especially true in the United States, where a traditionally diverse population now boasts even greater diversity. As populations diversify, so do their economic bases. In business and industry, national boundaries are vanishing as the world becomes an interconnected marketplace. Perhaps the most remarkable evidence of this trend is the European Union, which is building an economically unified Western Europe, complete with a single currency to replace the various national currencies. Given European history in the 20th century, this manifestation of globalization is amazing in many ways; but it also can be seen as emblematic of the global village of the 21st century.

In the United States increased international competition for consumer goods, technology, energy, and labor directly affects the country's economic health. For example, foreign companies are buying or investing in U.S. corporations, U.S. companies are using imported parts for their products, and some American companies are relocating manufacturing plants to countries with lower labor costs. Asian and American companies have entered into partnerships to produce automobiles and other consumer goods. The protectionist slogan, "Buy American," is hard to live by in a time when most complex goods contain components from the United States and abroad, regardless of their final point of manufacture. In fact, during the 1990s the United States ceased to be *the* dominant economic power and became more of a partner in the global marketplace.

New technology enables people to exchange ideas, services, and information almost instantaneously and on a global scale. Anyone who possesses a radio or a television with a satellite link can receive news about politics, the arts, the sciences, sports, and medicine as it is developing anywhere in the world. Computers linked to the Internet are allowing individuals, schools, and businesses not only to receive information but also to interact with it. The "connected" computer user can respond to ideas through news groups, mailings lists, and chat rooms. Today almost every aspect of life has a universal context. Concerns about crime, disease, and the environment that previously were considered local matters now have global significance; and solving such specific problems as drug trafficking, AIDS, and global warming will require worldwide cooperation and shared responsibility.

Global Education

As new international realities displace traditional notions about geography, politics, and economics, educators must respond with global education for students at all levels. In the United States much of the typical school curriculum remains nationalistic, provincial, and ethnocentric. American students often have difficulty locating continents on a globe, let alone the countries on the continents. Few U.S. students develop fluency in a foreign language, while most of their counterparts in other countries are literate in at least two languages. Student knowledge of foreign cultures tends to be sparse, because instead of presenting an accurate, up-to-date view of an interconnected planet, the curriculum too often presents a picture of a world that no longer exists.

The primary objective of global education is to prepare students for productive citizenship in the emerging global environment. In his satirical work, *The Saber-Tooth Curriculum*, Harold Benjamin, the first director of International Education Relations in the United States Office of Education, wrote about New-Fist, the designer of the first school curriculum.[2] New-Fist's curriculum included such topics as grabbing fish, clubbing woolly horses for food, and scaring saber-tooth tigers for protection. New-Fist's students who were educated in these subjects clearly had an advantage over those who were unschooled.

But as time passed, the world changed. With the approaching Ice Age, the streams became murky and it was impossible to see fish for fish grabbing; the woolly horses departed to warmer climates; and the saber-tooth tigers died. Thus the school curriculum became outdated and needed modification. Some education reformers suggested new subjects for meeting the needs of their changing world. These included making nets for catching fish in muddy streams, constructing snares for catching antelope instead of woolly horses, and digging pits on bear trails for protection from the glacial bears that arrived with the ice sheet. These activities required new knowledge and skills in order for people to survive. Unfortunately, the original curriculum was entrenched, and the school day was too crowded to introduce the new subjects.

The education atmosphere described in Benjamin's narrative can be observed in today's schools. Just as New-Fist's curriculum needed to be changed to reflect a changing world, so too does the typical school curriculum need to be revised in order to reflect present and likely future realities. The United States cannot stand aloof from events happening in other parts of the world. That world is no longer distant. To prepare students for our interconnected world, schools must develop a curriculum that 1) offers a global perspective in all subjects at all levels, 2) is extensive and international, and 3) is open to new ideas as they emerge. Instead of focusing too tightly on innumerable facts, global education requires discerning the "big ideas" and applying the pertinent facts. The emphasis is on developing the thinking skills needed to solve global problems and to adjust to new circumstances.

Just as the survival of New-Fist's people depended on teaching them new content that reflected their new realities, so today's teachers and curriculum developers face the same challenge of providing students with knowledge about the current global environment so they can become productive citizens of their world.

Global education also should prepare students to understand and to work with people from cultures other than their own. One step toward achieving this objective is a recommendation of the National Commission on Social Studies that advocates combining United States and world history. By providing an international, cross-cultural context for understanding the history of the United States, students would both better understand the international influences on the development of the nation and become more aware of other cultures as distinct entities. Such lessons would go beyond conventional classroom instruction.

The development and use of new technology in the classroom, especially during the last quarter of the 20th century, supports global education. In particular, the Internet is useful for teachers and students to assemble and examine resources from and about other countries and cultures. For example, students who are studying China can access a wide range of websites for information. These websites provide information about China's government, history, music, economy, religion, foreign policy, and education. As new websites are discovered, they can be bookmarked and linked for ready access whenever information is needed.

The Internet also offers ways to exchange information. Electronic mail — e-mail — enables students and teachers to communicate with their counterparts, friends, and families worldwide. Such communication can engender new forms of learning. For example, a popular Internet project is a bilingual newspaper. Students in Spanish classes in English-speaking countries collaborate with students in English classes in Spanish-speaking countries to write, edit, and publish (electronically or on paper) a bilingual newspaper. Students from both groups are encouraged to write in both languages as a way of developing fluency. The subject matter acquaints students with their counterparts' culture. And friendships made electronically often develop and last, sometimes with the students actually traveling to meet one another.

The Internet and related technology likely will become increasingly important in education in the 21st century. One has only to remember how quickly the computer, first, and later the Internet swept around the globe to realize that the rapid changes witnessed in the last quarter of the 20th century are not likely to diminish in the 21st. Anxiety over potential "Y2K" problems should be remembered as a tangible sign of the pervasive importance — even dependence in some quarters — on the computer and worldwide electronic linkage.

A structure for global education got impetus in 1976, when Robert Hanvey, writing for the Center for Teaching International Relations, advanced the following definition:

> Global education is learning about those issues that cut across national boundaries and about the interconnectedness of systems, ecological, cultural, economic, political, and technological. Global education involves perspective taking, seeing things through the eyes, minds, and hearts of others; and it means the realization that while individuals and groups may view life differently, they also have common needs and wants.[3]

Hanvey's definition implies more than adding a civics class, a foreign language class, or a social studies unit on international relations. The total curriculum should incorporate a global outlook, exposing students to the literature, art, music, and other features of different cultures.

In 1990, to help educators develop a global curriculum, the Global/International Education Commission of the Association for Supervision and Curriculum Development presented its global curriculum principles and model curricula. The principles include:

- All teachers, as well as students, should have opportunities to learn about and work with individuals whose ethnic and cultural backgrounds are different from their own.
- International/global studies should be viewed as cross-disciplinary, involving the arts, humanities, sciences, and mathematics, as well as foreign languages and social studies.
- The effect on individuals and on society of the increase in transnational interactions should be included in the curriculum, reflecting interdependence with other nations and the role of the United States in the global economy.
- The changing role of nations in the world system should be explained throughout the instructional materials, and the increasing number and importance of international organizations should be highlighted wherever appropriate.
- The changing and evolving role of the United States in world affairs should be included in the study of international trends and developments.[4]

Global education is not universally prized. Critics contend that global education will diminish patriotism and undermine national values. If the emphasis is on a world system and the increasing importance of international organizations, then the significance of one's own country begins to decline and local/national beliefs and values become less meaningful. This concern, always present to a degree, surfaced with new vigor late in the last century when, for example, some American soldiers serving in United Nations peacekeeping units objected to wearing the U.N. insignia and submitting themselves to command from officers of other countries. The soldiers believed that they swore allegiance only to the United States and thus it was not legitimate or part of their oath to obey orders issued by soldiers of other nations.

Diminished national sovereignty also can be illustrated by the willingness of some national governments, at least in some instances, to seek and then abide by decisions made by international entities, such as an international court. A trade decision by the United States, for example, might be questioned by one or more trading partners, with the resolution coming not from the United States but from the World Trade Organization.

Perhaps the most vivid example of diminished national sovereignty is the European Union, which coalesced in the late 20th century as an economic union, to the extent of having a single European currency to replace the various national currencies.

Proponents of global education point out that its intent is not to reject national beliefs or to diminish national sovereignty, but to better understand the beliefs of others.[5] Developing understanding should not cause a person to reject one's own country. In fact, the European Union often is cited as an example. Global education has been an intrinsic component of the European school curriculum for many years. Although there are many connections among European nations, such as free trade and a common currency, there is still a strong sense of national pride. Although European nations may share a currency, most believe that their patriotism and different social values will almost certainly prevent any future governmental or cultural merger.

Critics of global education also are concerned that students will be taught that all values and beliefs have equal worth or that instructors will instill into students ideals and standards contrary to those taught in the student's home. As the world becomes more interconnected, ideologies that were previously confined to a specific culture or location now become part of the public square and the collective national culture. These differing philosophies, when studied in school, may be presented as having the same or greater relevance than the culture's historically accepted beliefs. When students come home from school questioning the values of their home because they have been exposed to different beliefs in the classroom, many parents become concerned about how the global curriculum is presented.

There is no easy answer to this concern. Parents with firm social or religious beliefs often aver that the values and philosophy of their home are based on universal truths, and they desire that their children remain faithful to these beliefs. When teachers present a learning theory or classroom curriculum that motivates children to question the beliefs of their homes, the teachers are frequently accused of indoctrinating students or being hostile to the family.

Educators have addressed this issue by insisting that the legitimate role of teachers is to stimulate their students to learn and think about the global systems. Such study is not undertaken to tell them what to think or what conclusions they should draw from their new knowledge. For example, one issue that often is discussed as part of a global education curriculum concerns whether nations should disarm. All aspects of the topic should be discussed because one aim of education is to have students investigate and evaluate ideas. However, it is not appropriate for teachers to indoctrinate; and teachers should never insist that their students conform to a predetermined, "politically correct" answer regarding arguable issues.

When concerns such as these cannot be satisfactorily addressed in the parents' minds, one alternative to which parents can, and do, turn is private schooling or home schooling. Many parents who are dissatisfied with public schooling seek a narrower curriculum that they believe will be more in tune with their values. They often liken their children to new plants. Young plants must be cultivated and protected from the elements in a controlled environment, such as a greenhouse, in order to survive and grow strong. When the plants are hardy enough to survive, they may then be replanted in a unprotected environment. In a similar manner, children must be nurtured and protected from influences that conflict with the teachings in the home in order to grow strong. The home school or private school is the greenhouse that insulates the students from outside influences. Once students' values are firmly established, they can leave the "greenhouse" and enter the public square with the tools to defend their beliefs.

Critics of home schooling and narrowly focused, often church-based, private schools argue that these schools are indoctrinating students far more than any public school does. Yes, some public school teachers and education organizations do have a specific social agenda and do attempt to influence students. But in most cases, public school educators work hard to present straightforward information and to teach students to examine ideas and to draw their own conclusions. Most church-based schools and home schools, by their very nature, present only a single, highly specific worldview. The teachers in these schools specifically attempt to convince their students that this worldview is singularly correct.

Social arguments do not change the truth that today's world is a connected place and that all students need to have a global education in order to understand current issues and events. Students in the United States should not be detached from events happening in other parts of the world. The political, social, cultural, and economic realities of the 21st century demand that all schools offer a curriculum that presents a global perspective in all subjects and at all levels. This need is as valid for privately educated young people as it is for the students enrolled in public schools.

Only when students experience a curriculum with a global perspective will they be prepared to live and work in this interconnected world. They will be able to integrate their national history with world history, thus giving the study of history a global perspective. They will learn to understand people from other cultures and will develop loyalty to the interests of their own planet, as well as to the interests of their own nation. Finally, they will be able to live and work with people throughout the world, sharing new perspectives as they explore new choices and possibilities.

Notes

1. Marshall McLuhan and Bruce R. Powers, *The Global Village: Transformations in World Life and Media in the 21st Century* (New York: Oxford University Press, 1989).

2. Harold Benjamin, *The Saber-Tooth Curriculum* (New York: McGraw-Hill, 1939).
3. Robert G. Hanvey, *An Attainable Global Perspective* (Denver: Center for Teaching International Relations, 1976), p. 163.
4. Charlotte C. Anderson, with Susan K. Nicklas and Agnes R. Crawford, *Global Understandings: A Framework for Teaching and Learning* (Arlington, Va.: Association for Supervision and Curriculum Development, 1994), pp. 2-11.
5. Steven Hughes, "Multiple Views: Valuing Diversity," *Social Studies Review* 37 (Spring-Summer 1998): 15-17.

Chapter 3

The Global Curriculum

During the 20th century many attempts have been made to reform or change the general curriculum of American schools. In some instances a new program or system has been hastily incorporated into the curriculum, but these methods usually do not endure. One example is the TEMAC, or "teaching machine" method, of providing instruction in algebra that was attempted in the mid-1960s. In this method, students worked through a two-column algebra text at their own pace by filling in the blanks of incomplete sentences or working problems located in the left column. The answers in the right column were covered by a plastic sheet that the student would slide down the page to reveal the correct answers at the appropriate time. A teacher was in the classroom, but only to answer questions that the students might have. After a few semesters, TEMAC ceased to exist.[1] Similar self-paced instruction methods and devices met a similar fate.

Reform is more than a publisher's hot new product or the latest education fad. It is change that increases student learning and better prepares students for the world in which they will live as adults. When meaningful change does happen in the curriculum, it frequently comes as an incremental process linked to changes in society. Some examples involve teaching about the contributions of minorities, the use of computer-based technology in the classroom, and the establishment of learning communities. In each of these cases, the curriculum change was reinforced by widespread societal changes; and slowly but methodically the new idea or strategy became not just an addition to the curriculum, but an integral part of the instruction.

To illustrate this type of real reform, it might be well to consider the American history books of the 1960s. Almost all of the narratives in these textbooks just past mid-century were about the contributions of white males. The history of minorities and women usually were ignored. But beginning in that decade and extending through the final third of the 20th century, the civil rights and women's rights movements made American society more aware of the significance of minorities and women in American history. Initially, books specializing in presenting the accomplishments of women and minorities were published to be used as supplemental classroom materials. But as time passed, the principal history textbooks began to incorporate information about women and minorities into their narratives and to present a more complete story of U.S. history. Change in this area is still continuing, as some educators believe that history textbooks are still deficient concerning the inclusion of minority groups.[2]

The Impetus for Globalism

The introduction of a global curriculum has the ingredients for meaningful change. It is supported by changes in society, it will better prepare students for the world in which they will live as adults, and it has the potential to increase learning. The United States was forged by people of different cultures; and during the latter part of the 20th century, American society became increasingly diverse as people arrived from Asia and Latin America. Higher birthrates among some ethnic minorities led to increasing percentages of minorities in schools. All of this increased the perception of diversity. At the same time, minority social awareness increased and there arose new calls to preserve cultural diversity. The "American metaphor" for diversity changed from the melting pot to the patchwork quilt. The same is now occurring in many

Americans' views of the world. Shrunk by global economics and high-speed transportation and communications, the time has come for serious attention to a global curriculum.

Many teachers are quick to understand the reasons for curriculum reform and what reforms are needed. The problem is implementation. Fortunately, resources for incorporating global education into the curriculum can be found almost everywhere: in classroom texts and resource materials, in the local community, on CD-ROM databases, and on the Internet. Because global education corresponds with the realities in society, providing classroom experiences with a global perspective does not need to be forced into the curriculum. It can easily be made an integral part of most studies. For example, most public school classrooms nowadays include students from a variety of cultures. These students and their families often can provide a wealth of information when teaching with a global perspective. For a simple example in an English, geography, or social studies class, some teachers have asked their students to write about an aspect of their home culture. These papers can be presented orally and later bound into a classroom book. Or the stories can be printed in a classroom newspaper for distribution throughout the school and even to parents. This type of assignment enables all students to discover facts about their own cultures and to learn about the cultures of their peers.[3]

Members of students' families who have special knowledge, skills, or talents that will add a global perspective to the curriculum being studied frequently are invited to make presentations to the class. This involves more parents with the school and helps the students better understand the cultures of their classmates and the contributions of those cultures. In a mathematics class, a subject not often designed to have a global component, presentations by parents from different cultures illustrate to the students how many cultures have influenced the development of present-day mathematics. For example, in one case, an African-American parent presented information about algebra from the Rhind papyrus, an Egyptian treatise on mathematics dating from 1650 B.C.

Perhaps the information that most interests students is when they discover that some of the algebra problems found on the Rhind papyrus are almost identical to problems in modern algebra books. During another class, a Hindu parent talked about Aryabhata the Elder, a mathematician from India who wrote a summary of Hindu mathematics in verse form during the late 400s. The work included correct formulas for the area of a circle and a triangle; however, the formulas for the volumes of a sphere and a pyramid were incorrect. Other knowledge contained in the work of Aryabhata included information about quadratic equations, continued fractions, and power series.

The diversity in today's classrooms provides teachers with occasions to develop cooperative learning strategies that enable students from one culture to share ideas and perspectives with students from other cultures. An assignment from an American history class that incorporates a cooperative learning strategy concerns how the United States treated the Cherokee Indians during the early part of the 1800s. The teacher first organizes the students into small heterogeneous groups and then asks each group to form and present a consensus opinion regarding how ethically the Cherokees were treated by the United States in the circumstances leading up to the Trail of Tears. By requiring agreement, the students are compelled to explore each event and its consequences. Often the students become engaged in powerful and persuasive discussions, but they are being prepared for successful global cooperation and competition. When groups are unable to reach consensus, they should be permitted to present both a majority and a minority opinion.[4]

Projects and Resources

Other meaningful instructional projects and resources for a global curriculum include people and organizations found in the local community and beyond. Every locale has libraries, museums, businesses, churches, civic groups, and other types of organizations that are connected to other peoples and nations either locally or through their national affiliates. Some of these groups even have designed curriculum guides and materials that are available at little or no cost. For example, on the national level the World Affairs Council Network and the Peace Corps provide access to information for teaching global education. The World Affairs Council (online at www.worldaffairs.org/GEO.html) is an organization committed to promoting a greater understanding of international affairs. Using the council's resources, teachers from member schools are able to request classroom presentations by international students and scholars, a United Nations field trip for their class, or professional development seminars. International speakers provide local students with a personalized view of the speaker's country and culture and often evoke stimulating cross-cultural exchanges. Similarly, the Peace Corps (www.peacecorps. gov/wws/index.html) has developed a World Wise Schools program that includes returned volunteers who will make presentations at local schools or correspond with the students. Other World Wise Schools educator resources include lesson plans categorized by grade level and subject area, teacher guides, and videos.

Community resources for speakers with international experience are usually plentiful. Often, a call to local businesses results in finding people who have traveled overseas on company business and are willing to give talks about the countries they have visited. In most areas, travel agents are an abundant source of global information. Not only are travel agents well versed about many cultures and countries, they often have access to videos, travel documentation, and posters. Another resource that often is overlooked is the church. Most congregations support missionary and humanitarian efforts in other countries. When one of these individuals comes to visit locally, he or she may be willing to make a presentation at the school. Often these people work with the foreign populace more closely than do those in business and industry and thus are able to paint a more accurate picture of the other culture.

Another group with cross-cultural experiences and instructional resources is the teachers themselves. Many teachers have studied or taught overseas, participated in international projects, lived overseas while in the military, or simply traveled to various countries. When teaching from a global perspective, it often is beneficial to survey local teachers and identify their cross-cultural experiences. Sometimes a souvenir can be the catalyst for an informative classroom experience. One instance concerned a geography teacher who was presenting a unit about Australia and had a colleague who just returned from a honeymoon in Australia. Although the colleague did not venture too far from her resort hotel, she did buy several mementos. One was a didjeridu, a musical instrument made from a eucalyptus branch and used by the Australian aborigines. Working with the music teacher, the geography teacher developed a unit on traditional Australian music, during which each student attempted to play the didjeridu.

Locally, teachers can work with members of community groups to create global units for the school curriculum. In one city a curriculum writing team from a local middle school and the assistant director of the local historical museum designed a project that used the museum's exhibit about how people from a variety of cultures helped to develop the area. First, the students heard presentations from people of different cultures who grew up in the local community. These individuals told about experiences from their childhood. Then the students visited the museum, where the exhibits illustrated how the various cultures transformed the area. In this case, students learned about the contributions of Native Americans, Germans, Moravians, African Americans, and Jews. After the museum visit, the students created projects that illustrated what they had learned. The projects included making pottery with modeling clay, constructing maize necklaces and bracelets, writing folk stories, creating posters, and preparing ethnic foods.

In addition to local historical and cultural museums, other community resource sites that may be incorporated into a global curriculum include the local arboretum and zoo. One science class project had students identify and classify trees, vines, grasses, and other plants at the arboretum. After studying the plants, the students used a world map to locate the countries in which the plants were native. A stimulating part of the science class trip was using the setting as a background for a global activity that involved another discipline, English. The science teacher obtained some examples of Japanese haiku from the English teacher and had the students recite the haikus under a vine trellis in the arboretum. Similar projects may be incorporated into a science class by using animals at the local zoo. For example, as part of an assignment in which students are studying the characteristics of mammals on display at the zoo, the students can use a world map to indicate the range for each of the animals.

Advantages of Teaching Globally

When rendering knowledge about the numerous cultures in the global community, many disciplines are involved. Teachers and resources provide information about an area's history, customs, arts, current events, language, and other topics. Instead of each class presenting fragmented information, educators should work together to develop lessons that use the skills and learning from several disciplines. The curriculum should be purposely linked so that the students will find greater coherence in what they are learning. One example is an activity that integrates geography, English, art, music, foreign language, and multicultural education. Students in an English class read the book, *Follow the Drinking Gourd*, by Jeanette Winter. The object of the lesson is to help students understand what slaves were forced to endure when they were in bondage and what they were willing to risk to be free. After reading the book, students write a paper about the hardships the slaves endured and the dangers of trying to escape; and then students make an oral presentation to the class. The students translate part of their paper as an assignment in their foreign language class. In geography class, the students use a map of the underground railroad, Winter's book, and an atlas to find places mentioned in the book and to determine escape routes. Finally, the students draw or paint a scene from the book and learn a song of the period.

Global perspective projects such as this one enable students to progress beyond the skill of learning factual knowledge to the reasoning skills of problem solving and critical thinking. Educators and cognitive scientists use the terms *associative strategies* or *higher-order skills* to describe the skills of students who think and read critically, find information, and solve problems using metacognitive strategies. In the assignment using Winter's book, the students read the material to discover information. They then analyze and synthesize what they read to write their paper. And finally they defend what they wrote during the oral presentation. Mapping the underground railroad also requires that the students proceed beyond the facts presented in the book and use a variety of cognitive strategies to determine the route of the underground railroad.

The characteristics of a global curriculum also encourage holistic learning. In a holistic learning environment, assignments are constructed about real-world problems and projects, instead of the standard subject matter disciplines. For example, after reading Winter's book about the underground railroad, the students could discuss prejudice in the United States and other countries. This is an issue that often is discussed outside the classroom and has a real-world context that directly affects each student. Discussing prejudice in other countries demonstrates the universality of the problem and that people from various cultures also are victims. This and similar holistic assignments increase students' motivation because students can recognize and sometimes experience the relevance of the assignment. Life, itself, becomes a teacher.

Finally, global-based projects, especially those that encourage holistic learning, enable teachers to evaluate their students using performance-based assessments. In performance-based assessments, student learning is evaluated by using an assignment or a project similar to ones that would be required in the world outside the classroom. These types of global projects may include, but are not limited to, publishing a bilingual newspaper; writing fables, poetry, or short stories based on the experiences of different cultures; constructing a museum exhibit; or developing a guidebook to help a person from another country become a U.S. citizen. For each of these projects, students are required to integrate knowledge from several disciplines; and teachers should stress this integration among the disciplines. Student motivation is increased because the project is practical and based on a global reality, and the assessment illustrates a benefit of education.

Notes

1. P. Saettler, *A History of Instructional Technology* (New York: McGraw-Hill, 1968).
2. Carl A. Grant and William F. Tate, "Multicultural Education Through the Lens of the Multicultural Education Research Literature," in *Handbook of Research on Multicultural Education*, edited by J.A. Banks and C.A. Banks (New York: Macmillan, 1995). ERIC No. ED382704.
3. Barbara J. Diamond and Margaret A. Moore, *Multicultural Literacy: Mirroring the Reality of the Classroom* (White Plains, N.Y.: Longman, 1995). ERIC No. ED376444.
4. Dan Wishnietsky, *Brooks Global Studies Extended-Year Magnet School* (Bloomington, Ind.: Phi Delta Kappa International, 1996).

Chapter 4

Technology and the Global Curriculum

Students today live in a society in which computer-based technology has become far-reaching. When the first personal computers were unveiled in the 1970s, few people recognized the profound effect computers and computer-based technology would have on society. Not only did technology proliferate into all areas of business, industry, and education, but the U.S. economy shifted from an industrial society to an information society. Between 1950 and 1990 the percent of people in the workforce involved in some manner with the information industry jumped from 17% to about 70%. Currently, almost every American worker has some involvement. The information industry, which accounted for 3.3% of the gross national product in 1985 and approximately 6.1% of the GNP in 1993, is now the world's largest industry.[1]

Computer-based technologies have quickly become one of the powerful forces molding society. From their homes, people are using their computers to access Internet resources, pay monthly bills, analyze the stock market, make hotel and airline reservations, submit tax returns, and do many other useful activities. Hospital computers are helping doctors diagnose diseases and recommend treatments; geologists use computers to predict possible locations of mineral deposits; and air freight companies use computers to track packages. In virtually all areas of business and industry, computers are an essential part of corporate operating procedure. For many, it was as if God said, "Let there be computer-based technology," and there was. Seemingly without notice or warning, this unknown machine became an integral part of our worldwide culture.

Technology also has proliferated into all areas of schools. Almost every campus now has computers in administrative offices, classrooms, and libraries or learning centers. During the 1980s and 1990s, educators were trained to use microcomputers, computer software was developed for almost every discipline, and students were introduced to computing. However, the accomplishments from the 20th century were just a foundation for the technological advances that are currently transpiring and will occur in the future. Although no one can predict the future with perfect certainty, it is reasonable to expect that technology will become increasingly more powerful, productive, and accessible in the workplace, in the home, on the campus, and in the classroom. As technology becomes more universal, powerful, and flexible, the challenge for educators is to design curricula that provide additional opportunities to enhance learning by creating an atmosphere in which all students may achieve their full potential.

Integrating Technology into Curricula

The integration of technology and education is not a new phenomenon. For example, a machine invented almost six centuries ago, the printing press with movable type, is what enables every student to have printed textbooks, still the most often used teaching aid. Other technological changes that have influenced education over the years include the use of blackboards, stereoscopes, overhead projectors, ballpoint pens, slide rules, and calculators. These and other changes in school technology emerged gradually and caused only modest changes in the curriculum. The current evolution of computer-based technologies is different. Instead of deliberate and uncomplicated, the development of the computer has been rapid and complex. This has created considerable apprehension among many teachers who complain that they are offered inadequate inservice training on the new technology, even as their school is being equipped with the latest hardware and software.

The "peopleware" component when incorporating computer-based technology is as essential to the system as is the hardware and software. When microcomputers were first introduced into the schools, many teachers were concerned that they would be replaced by a machine. Instead of superseding the teacher, computers illustrated the importance of competent teachers who could design meaningful learning environments. Just incorporating technology into the classroom does not automatically increase learning; in fact, sometimes learning decreases. It is the classroom teacher who must evaluate the technology to determine if it is well designed and pedagogically sound, if it will strengthen the curriculum, and if and how it should be incorporated. Without this type of teacher involvement, the best-designed technology and software applications will do little to increase learning.

It is puzzling when school administrators spend thousands of dollars for computer hardware and software and then fail to invest in staff development. Why buy the technology if there are no people who know how to use it? Although there are several approaches to staff development, a model that is cost-effective and provides sufficient technological understanding for teachers is a program that develops in-house experts. The in-house experts are the teachers or administrators in a local school who have an interest in computers and desire to learn more about computer-based technology and how to incorporate this technology into the curriculum. Administrators can provide support through release time and remuneration. After being selected, the designated teachers attend a series of workshops that not only teach the technology but also provide participants with hands-on learning so that they will experience how technology contributes to instructional development and increased learning. The new experts then become the resource people for their school who can help incorporate technology into the curriculum and educate other teachers in its use.

Teachers also must take responsibility for becoming proficient using the available computers and computer-based technologies. Regardless of whether administrative support is adequate or lacking, classroom instructors cannot ignore the importance of technology in the curriculum. People who have the intelligence and competence to become teachers also have the capability to learn independently how to use the new technologies. Because they demand the finest curriculum for their students, many faculty members have taught themselves necessary computer literacy when there was a lack of administrative support. There are books, classes at local colleges and universities, seminars at professional conferences, and articles in professional journals that provide the required information. Obviously, it is preferable to have the school system's support; but when that does not occur, teachers should take the initiative and learn the needed skills.

A Short History

The initial computers used in classrooms during the 1980s were quite primitive by current standards. The system usually had one disk drive for storing information on a floppy disk and, at most, 64 kilobytes of internal, or random access, memory (RAM). In addition, school computers were isolated from each other or connected with only the other computers in the same room. The first educational software programs were equally basic, usually consisting of drill-and-practice sessions or tutorials. A few of these software programs included some rudimentary sound or graphics, but a majority were limited to text. In general, the early computers had monochrome monitors, limited sound capability, and slow processing speed; and they were used only for word-processing applications, creating databases or spreadsheets, and computer-assisted review sessions.

By the 1990s computers and their accompanying technology had become much more sophisticated. Instead of only one floppy disk drive for reading and storing limited amounts of data, the newer computer systems included hard drives that could save gigabytes of information and optical disc players for storing and retrieving vast quantities of audio, video, graphics, and text. Processing speed increased by more than tenfold. Monitors displayed an almost limitless number of color shades in a high-resolution display that rivaled a photograph. Audio capabilities included lifelike stereo reproductions of almost any sound, including speech and music. Random access memory increased from the 64 kilobytes to 64 megabytes and more. In terms of pages of text, this is equivalent to increasing the internal memory from approximately 16 pages of information to more than 16,000 pages.

Features also were added that made computers more user friendly to all students. One such feature, when activated, would magnify the size of the text or graphic on the monitor so students who were visually impaired could better view the information. The computer-assisted instruction advanced far beyond the drill-and-practice programs to simulations, problem solving, and discovery learning. With each successive upgrade in computer technology, the developers of educational software have been able to design and market more realistic educational software products.[2]

Examples of educational software products currently found in most schools are databases stored on optical disks. Using these disks and their computer, students are able to obtain information from encyclopedias, almanacs, atlases, dictionaries, and reference works. In addition to the text and pictures that can be found in the book format of these resources, the optical disk also includes full-motion color video, stereo sound, and animation. The amount of information that can be stored on today's optical disks is measured in gigabytes and is equivalent to the audio and video of a full-length feature film along with many thousands of pages of text or graphics. When displayed on a high-quality monitor, video from an optical disk can render a clearer picture than most VCRs.

Accessing the desired information is accomplished using the optical disk's internal search feature. Students seeking information about a topic simply type a word or a phrase that describes the subject matter, and a list of applicable articles, videos, graphics, and sounds is presented. Students can access information stored on a single frame or track of the optical disk, progressing forward or backward from that point or freezing the information on the computer's monitor. If the frame is a picture, it appears fixed on the screen. A helpful feature found on current optical disk databases is how relevant information is linked. For example, the words of an encyclopedia article might be linked to a dictionary, so when students do not know the meaning of a word, they double click it, and its definition appears on the screen. Some words or phrases are highlighted with a distinct feature to signify that they are linked to a graphic, video, or sound. By double clicking the highlighted area, the multimedia feature is accessed.

In addition to databases, optical disks include instructional applications and simulations. One example is an electronic textbook about the human body. A student can examine a particular nerve or joint. One interactive feature of the program enables students to electronically stimulate the nerve being examined, and the computer will demonstrate how the nerve affects other body parts. By using the power of the computer, electronic textbooks advance beyond traditional text and pictures by providing a computer simulation of a scientific reality.

Other examples of optical disk-based interactive textbooks and applications are used in mathematics and foreign language classes. One feature of a statistics electronic textbook illustrates how data from actual experiments will result in a certain distribution. In one instance, the textbook randomly selects the weights at birth of 10, 100, and 1,000 full-term baby girls. When the data is plotted as a relative frequency histogram, the curve better approximates a normal distribution as the size of the sample increases. An example of a computer-based application used in foreign language classes is language translation programs. These programs will translate words either from the home language to the language being learned or vice versa to help students reinforce their foreign language vocabulary. Another application that also reinforces foreign language vocabulary is an application that presents the same text in more than one language. Many of these optical disks also have a computer-generated voice that will aid the students' pronunciation skills.

Networking and the Internet

Perhaps the most important area of computer-based technology that has influenced education was the development and introduction of the Internet. Consisting of millions of computers connected by high-speed data lines, the Internet enables students and teachers to extend beyond the classroom by communicating with people and accessing resources located throughout the world. The idea for what was to become the Internet was formed in 1956 after the U.S.S.R. launched Sputnik. To help strengthen science and technology, a division of the Department of Defense proposed the formation of a computer-based communication network that would allow all types of computers to communicate with each other using a common language. The beginnings of the network became a reality in 1969 when three computers were connected by telephone lines. As early as 1984 the number of computers on the network totaled more than a thousand.

During the 1980s a major change occurred in computing. Many applications that previously required a large mainframe could now be performed on a small and relatively inexpensive desktop computer. Soon, computing power moved from the mainframe in the locked room to the desk of the teacher and student. By connecting these desktop computers to the network, all members of the scholastic community began to gain access to the network resources. In 1986 the National Science Foundation established a powerful computer network to handle the increasing number of users. Less-expensive computers and easier network access caused continued growth, and within a short period of time the data lines of the National Science Foundation were joined with the data lines of major communications companies. The modern Internet was a reality.

The first K-12 schools were connected to the Internet in 1988, and by 1994 more than a thousand secondary schools were online. Currently, most educators have access to Internet resources through their school or through a computer and modem in their home. In fact, any person with a computer, modem, and a phone or cable line is able to connect to the Internet by subscribing to a commercial online service or an Internet service provider. Recognizing that technology was becoming an important part of society, the U.S. Congress passed and President Bush signed the High-Performance Computing Act of 1991. One purpose of this bill was to create a federal program that would establish a National Research and Education Network that would ensure that all users would be able to transmit and receive data quickly and easily. As the Internet continued to became a more vital part of society and education, the federal government proceeded to fund initiatives during the 1990s and into this century to better incorporate technology into the curriculum. This became especially important, beginning in 1992, when World Wide Web technology became part of the Internet. Instead of just sending or receiving text, users of the Internet now could route graphics, audio, and video. Teachers, students, and others could readily access and retrieve online information located in libraries, museums, research facilities, organizations, government agencies, and the many other important databases located throughout the world.[3]

Most teachers now consider the Internet as essential a tool as the overhead projector, calculators, manipulatives, or even textbooks. As with any tool, the primary test occurs when teachers decide they can teach better with the tool than without it and when learning increases when the tool is employed. For example, science teachers in different countries might decide to design a project using the electronic mail feature of the Internet. Students would be assigned to collect data regarding the number of daylight hours on specific dates. Using the Internet, the students from each class would e-mail the other classes such needed information as the number of minutes of daylight for each date and the longitude and latitude of each location. After exchanging the data, each class would form conclusions about the relationships among the variables and then exchange their thoughts via the electronic network. Conclusions would be compared, and any disagreements could be resolved. In this example, the students benefit by collecting and using actual data, collaborating with students from other cultures, and using the Internet to communicate with each other.

Another feature of the Internet is its ability to quickly access an almost infinite number of resources. One perpetual complaint concerning traditional textbooks is that even if they were copyrighted this year, the information is often two or more years old. This is especially a problem when the textbook nears the end of the adoption cycle and may be eight or ten years old. For example, a world geography text may have a map of the Middle East that has borders that are long out of date. Although teachers may not be able to buy newer textbooks with the correct information, they can use Internet resources to provide students with a current map of the area and information about individual countries and each country's history.

Teachers also can use Internet resources to provide students with information as it is occurring. For example, when space probes send pictures to NASA, the pictures often are available on the Internet within days or hours of being received. These pictures are not there only for researchers, but are made available to any student or teacher with an Internet connection. Similar illustrations can be found in every discipline as teachers discover that resources of the information highway are an invaluable way to ensure that students are presented with the most current information available.

How Can the Internet Best Be Used?

With the many resources available online, most educators would agree that the Internet and the World Wide Web are meaningful resources for learning and should be incorporated into the classroom. The concern for many teachers is how to embrace these resources and make them an integral part of the curriculum. Although the Internet is a relatively new resource, deciding how it should be established in the curriculum is similar to procedures involving the more traditional resources. For example, a teacher might want to assemble resources to update or fill gaps in the current textbook. One method would be to have a supplementary reading list of books and articles that the students would read. By using Internet technology, however, the teacher could provide the same information by presenting the students with a list of appropriate websites. Instead of finding a number of books and articles, the student would use a computer connected to the Internet, access the listed webpages, and retrieve the information. An increasing number of teachers are creating their own webpage with a list of the assigned websites. By using the "link" feature of the World Wide Web, the teacher can associate each item of the list with a hyperlink that will connect the student directly to the listed webpage. The student simply accesses the teacher's webpage and clicks the item on the list, and the desired webpage is displayed.

Another method of employing Internet resources in the curriculum is to assemble a virtual multimedia collage about a certain topic. Suppose, for example, the topic being studied is black history in the United States. The teacher would compose a webpage that would have links to maps, photographs, sound and video files, quotations, and relevant data. Specific links could include a map of the underground railroad; photographs of Sojourner Truth, Frederick Douglas, and Martin Luther King; sound and video clips of civil rights speakers; quotations from the Civil Rights Act; and articles giving different opinions about affirmative action. By placing the links in chronological order, students could effectively comprehend the consequence of history and how the past influences the present.

Instead of the teacher assembling resources, the students could be assigned a topic and asked to discover Internet resources and to answer questions about the subject. The students would use one or more of the major search engines to locate websites relating to the topic and to develop their own knowledge base using

Internet resources. When the instructors prepare well-designed questions, the students become involved in solving problems, interpreting material, and evaluating beliefs. This is especially apparent when students work with one another and have to justify their evaluations. When students complete assignments individually, they too often merely accumulate facts, and any evaluations go uncontested. Students who complete the assignment with other classes, especially if the different classes are from other cultures, can find their beliefs challenged.

This is perhaps the most powerful teaching aspect of the Internet, enabling students to share perspectives, ideas, and projects with other students from around the globe. In most instances the first one or two sessions are devoted to teaching students how to access the Internet and communicate with other students. The class then selects a project and, in collaboration with several other classrooms, forms a global learning team. Each class develops its own assignments and communicates information and ideas with the other members of their team. Through e-mail, the students discuss their beliefs and attempt to resolve differences of opinion. The group's conclusions about the chosen topic are presented in a finished product, such as a team paper or project.

Suppose, for example, students are given the task of evaluating the current U.S. Administration's policy regarding the Middle East. The teacher, instead of presenting the assignment only to her class, has contacted teachers living in Israel, Egypt, Jordan, Great Britain, the United States, and Australia by using the Internet. By design, all of the teachers give their class the assignment and, in addition, all evaluations are e-mailed to all of the other classes. Each class then evaluates the opinions of the others. Because it is likely that the different classes will have conflicting opinions about how the situation in Palestine should be handled, each group then has to e-mail the other groups the rationale for their conclusions. This type of assignment truly places an international perspective on a global concern and forces the students not only to build knowledge and to form an opinion about an actual circumstance, but also to evaluate the beliefs of others and to justify their own convictions. It is not unusual for students to modify radical views because of this type of assignment.

Before attempting to incorporate the Internet into the curriculum, there are issues and concerns that should be resolved. One important element for teachers is the time it takes to plan and implement a meaningful curriculum. Finding appropriate websites and Internet resources is not a simple task. Even with today's powerful Internet search engines, creating a website list or a multimedia collage about a certain topic can require several hours. And still the work is not complete. The World Wide Web is always changing, and so teachers must verify the content and address of each listed website before each use. A website may not be updated regularly, or it may cease to exist entirely. Effective school administrators understand the importance of providing sufficient time for curriculum development. To use their time efficiently, teachers often will work in groups to search the Internet and develop lists of applicable resources and projects. It is a widespread practice for teachers when attending professional conferences to distribute and receive Internet resource lists from their colleagues.

As is the case with any resource, verification and evaluation are essential. Teachers should evaluate Internet-based information before incorporating it into the curriculum. Many educators spend a considerable amount of time evaluating texts, journal articles, and other sources of knowledge before deciding the materials to use in the classroom. Using Internet resources requires teachers to perform the same type of evaluation that they use when examining more traditional resources. Just because data is in print does not make it true, accurate, or valid. Similarly, information is not true, accurate, valid, or useful just because it is found on the Internet. Teachers and students should understand that this may be especially true of Internet resources. If a person with Internet access desires, he or she can post information to the network without any peer-evaluation process.

To use the Internet effectively and efficiently, both teachers and students require appropriate access to a connected computer. For teachers, this requires a computer connected to the Internet located in the instructor's office or some other easily accessible and private location. Most educators will not effectively use the Internet when it requires any effort that they believe should not be required. For example, many teachers will not walk to a computer lab to examine their e-mail on a daily basis, especially if they think there should be computers dedicated to teachers in an office or teachers' lounge. Another way to increase teacher use of the Internet is to provide computers for home use. Most schools do not have the funds to furnish each teacher with a dedicated computer for the home, but teachers should be permitted to bring a school computer home, especially when they are working on computer-based projects — particularly over the summer months and during vacation periods. Internet access from home can be provided through the telephone line or cable at nominal cost.

Students also require comprehensive access to Internet-connected computers if they are to learn how to use the Internet effectively. Most schools in the United States have computer labs or classroom-based computers that are connected to the Internet for student use. A problem occurs when there is limited availability. Often these student computers are in use during school hours, and students who depend on a school bus for transportation often do not have access before or after school. If the student's family has a home computer and subscribes to an Internet service provider, the school's computer is not essential; the student can work at home with his or her home computer and complete the assignment. However, many students' families cannot afford to purchase a home computer, and so public-access computers are required. One workable solution has been a partnership between the schools and area libraries. Computers with Internet access are located in practically every library. Thus the local library and the local school may be able to coordinate their assignments and schedules so that every student will have access. This has included extending library accessibility by using parents as volunteers in the library's computer lab.

Concerns About Inappropriate Internet Content

A growing concern among educators is the availability of "inappropriate" material on the Internet. Depending on definition, inappropriate resources on the Internet include such things as pornographic pictures, hate speech, and instructions for building and detonating explosives. These kinds of information are readily available to anyone who has access to the World Wide Web. Frequently, however, they are found by accident, rather than by intention. In one case, for example, a student performed an Internet search using "Venus" as the keyword. He was attempting to find a picture of the planet Venus. On the list of possible sites was a topless nightclub that had Venus in its name. Needless to say, the topless nightclub site would not be considered suitable for school use.

When students access Internet resources at school, they should be engaged in school-related work. Many schools closely monitor student use of the Internet to be certain that the computers are used in an appropriate manner, sometimes (but not always) specifically defining what is appropriate. Numerous schools designate a particular location, such as a media center or a dedicated computer lab, for their student-accessible computers that are connected to the Internet. When the computers are in one location, designated educators can observe the computer screens and monitor the sites that students are accessing. It also is possible to determine what sites are accessed by viewing the history file and temporary Internet files of the Internet browser. Individual teachers also can help with the monitoring process by carefully defining their Internet-related assignments and making sure the computer coordinator knows what the students should be doing on the computer.

Another method used by educators to limit student access to inappropriate sites is to obtain software programs that keep students from accessing certain Internet locations based on the content of the site or the site's address. To activate the software, the person responsible for maintaining the school computer network loads the program and sets the appropriate restrictions. One restriction used by educators is to deny student access to any webpage with certain sex-ually-oriented words. If students attempt to access a site deemed unsuitable, the computer screen simply displays a message that the location cannot be accessed.*

Regardless of how thorough educators are in trying to limit access to inappropriate sites, some students will be able to slip pass the censors. If governments and organizations cannot prevent unauthorized access to their computers, it is highly unlikely that the local school will be successful at preventing all student access to forbidden sites. Students also can conceal the websites they have visited by deleting their history and temporary Internet file with three or four clicks of the computer mouse. It seems a more reasonable course to suggest that 1) each school should develop clear policies regarding student use of the Internet and the conse-quences for violating such policies, and 2) students and parents should agree to the policy statement and sign it before the student is allowed to access the Internet on the school's computers.[4]

The Internet, like all other aspects of our Information Age society, has positives and negatives. Although the negative aspects cannot be fully avoided, schools must continue to prepare today's students for the technological environment that they will encounter as adults. The Internet will be a major part of that world. In all likelihood, students who do not know how to use technology will encounter problems in many areas and on many occasions. This does not mean that students will spend a majori-ty of their time on the Internet. Educators do not want students to become "mushrooms" by always using the computer and not see-ing the light of day. Virtual reality should not supersede real-world experiences. Educators must continually assess the pluses and minuses of our ever-changing technological landscape, for only by understanding computer-based technology will students be able to control it, integrate it into their lives, and use it well.

---

*For a discussion of legal issues surrounding such access, see Fred H. Cate's thought-provoking book, *The Internet and the First Amendment: Schools and Sexually Explicit Expression* (Phi Delta Kappa Educational Foundation, 1998).

Notes

1. Bureau of Labor Statistics, Bureau of the Census, *Current Population Survey*. www.blscensusv.gov./cps/cpsmain.htm
2. Jim Carlton, "It Seems Like Yesterday," *Wall Street Journal*, 16 November 1998, page R10.
3. Bard Williams, *The Internet for Teachers* (Forest City, Calif.: IDG Books Worldwide, 1995), pp. 9-28.
4. Wishnietsky, Dan H. *Internet Basics: An Educator's Guide to Traveling the Information Highway* (Bloomington, Ind.: Phi Delta Kappa Educational Foundation, 1997), pp. 54-55.

Chapter 5

Diversity
and Equity

The Internet and communicating with people in other countries and cultures are not essential for creating a global classroom environment. The diversity of students attending U.S. elementary and secondary schools indicates that a diverse classroom environment often already exists. Although many people presume that the school population consists of a white majority and a small ethnic/racial minority, the reality is that near the end of the 20th century the minority enrollment in grades one through 12 already was more than 35% and increasing. Some futurists predict, based on current trends, that at some point during the 21st century there will be an ethic majority group in the United States. This already has occurred in California. By the mid-1990s, less than 50% of the state's population was classified as "Anglo." This trend also was seen in California's schools. For example, in the San Diego City and County schools, the increase of minority students caused white student enrollment to fall below 50% as of 1994.[1]

The ethnic makeup encountered in the classroom is comparable to the ethnic structure of society as a whole because the United States, unlike many other countries, strives to educate all of its citizens. This has not always been the case. During the Colonial period, before the common school movement, only children from affluent homes were educated. The common school movement provided educational opportunities regardless of economic status, but not regardless of ethnic status. Until the latter part of the 20th century, mainstream public education was geared toward only the white middle class. Minorities often were seen as inferior and unteachable, and so trying to educate them was viewed by some as a waste of public funds. For example, when they were allowed to attend school, black students usually were educated separately from whites; and even as recently as the 1940s it was not uncommon for states to spend five times as much money to educate a white student as a black student.[2] This reality repeated itself for students from other racial backgrounds, especially Native American children. As late as 1980, only 50% of Native American children graduated from high school.[3] Fortunately, today there is a concerted effort among educators to meet the needs of all young people, regardless of economic status or ethnic background, though many negative stereotypes regarding minorities still exist.

Beyond Ethnicity

Ethnic difference was not the only inherited attribute that influenced how a student was perceived by the education system. Until recently, whether a student was male or female had a major effect on how and what he or she was taught. Females were believed to be mentally inferior to males. This view not only was a conventionalized idea held by the general public, it also became part of the scientific literature. For example, a medical text written in the late 19th century maintained that the development of the sex organs and the development of the brain were at opposite poles of the nervous system. Because the female reproductive system was more complex than that of the male, it required more nervous system energy to develop. This took place at the expense of the brain, with the result that the male was more intelligent than the female. There was even a warning that if a female were to educate herself and develop her intellect, the strain on her body would cause her to have a nervous breakdown or to become sterile.[4] Although most people would laugh at this belief today, for most of the 20th century females were educated in the "female" disciplines, such as teaching and nursing, and discouraged from becoming engineers or doctors. The current environment has greatly changed. Females are fully represented in many formerly "male" areas, such as medical schools, and usually are encouraged by educators to enter the field of their choice.

In addition to inherent differences, external factors, such as family traits, can greatly influence a student's learning environment. Family traits include such factors as parents' level of education, employment status, involvement with their child's education, overall support of local educators, and the home environment. From 1970 to the end of the century, the percent of parents with a high school diploma or its equivalent increased from about 60% to 85%. However, the percentages differ considerably among the various ethnic groups. For example, approximately 92% of white mothers had at least a high school diploma or equivalent in the late 1990s, compared to 78% of African-American mothers and 45% of Hispanic mothers. A positive trend is evident as parents' level of education continues to increase for all ethnic groups. This increase in level of education also has enhanced the employment status of many parents, especially those in the ethnic minority communities.[5]

Not all trends into the new century have been positive. Although the level of parents' education has increased, there also has been an increase in problematic parental behaviors and attitudes, which often have a negative effect on students. One example is the increasing number of parents who are not involved in their child's education. Lack of involvement is not always caused by a lack of interest. In many cases, increased time required by their job and increases of other life stresses prevent parents from being active in school-related matters. However, some parents also exhibit behaviors that are overtly harmful to their children. For example, the number of reported cases of parents who had problems with drug or alcohol abuse and the number of abused children greatly increased since the 1980s. Just over 900,000 children were victims of abuse and neglect in 1998. About 50% of the cases were neglect, 25% physical abuse, and 14% sexual abuse. There were 1,100 deaths. Based on statistics from the

Department of Health and Human Services, the number of children that were at risk more than doubled between 1988 and 1998.[6] Instability at home has a negative influence not only on individual students' education, but also on the students' collective well-being. Many organizations are attempting to intervene, both to help troubled families solve their problems and to ensure the safety and well-being of at-risk children.

Addressing Diversity-Based Education Needs

Many other variables could be cited to differentiate students in the classroom. Regardless of differences, the challenge for educators is to address the various abilities and learning styles and to provide an environment in which all students can succeed. This endeavor, to achieve a successful classroom environment, primarily hinges on the leadership of each and every teacher. It is the teacher who ultimately defines the classroom environment and interacts with students.

The need for leadership at the classroom level was recognized in the National Educational Goals Report of 1994, which stated that by the year 2000 teachers will be provided with the skills necessary to prepare all students for the 21st century.[7] Although there has been effort and even modest success toward attaining this goal through inservice and preservice education, considerable effort still is required to prepare teachers for teaching diverse populations of students.

A major responsibility for educators is to provide for each student a curriculum and a classroom atmosphere that is based on cultural realities, instead of exaggerations, stereotypes, or misconceptions. If teachers apply certain beliefs and preconceptions about a group to every member of that group, the learning environment and student outcomes will be influenced negatively. For example, one conventionalized idea about African Americans was that the achievement of black students will always be lower than that of white students, regardless of efforts to improve their performance. This belief was demonstrated to be incorrect. Several studies have illustrated that when there is quality teaching, high academic expectations for all children, and parent involvement, the academic attainment of African-American students equals or surpasses the national average. Many African Americans place great importance on formal education and believe it is a means for personal advancement and community improvement. This is often noticed at college graduations when everyone in the black graduate's extended family is in attendance, especially when the student graduating is the first in the family to earn a degree.[8]

Many other cultural stereotypes exist that promote false beliefs not only about African Americans, but also about Hispanics, Asians, Native Americans, and other ethnic minorities. These include myths regarding the family structure, innate intelligence, and past history. For example, many think that within all minority communities there is a high degree of instability in the family structure caused by a high rate of children born into single-parent homes and the absence of fathers. Among Latinos, the reality is just the opposite. When compared to all other ethnic groups, Latino families are more likely to have the traditional family structure of mother, father, and children. In addition, Latino families demonstrate a high commitment to strong family values based on a Christian worldview.[9]

Stereotypes sometimes appear positive and uplifting, but even these may cause difficulties. A common belief about Asian/Pacific Islander students is that they are intelligent and highly motivated and should excel in mathematics and the sciences. It is true that many Asian students do excel, but there are many students from all ethnic groups that are successful in school. Because of the stereotype that all Asians do well, educators frequently are slower to intervene when an Asian student is having academic or social problems. But Asian students' problems can be as severe as those of any other student. For example, a 1993 study conducted by the Centers for Disease Control and Prevention discovered that 45.6% of female Filipino students living in San Diego had seriously considered suicide within the previous year.[10] The stereotype can lead educators to miss these problems, with serious consequences for the students.

Perhaps the worst type of cultural stereotyping is one that eliminates a group's ethnic culture and existence. Some think that Native Americans were living in what is now the United States during the time of Colonial expansion, but they were not able to adjust with the times and, today, only an insignificant number are left. The truth is that there are approximately two million Native Americans living in the United States from more than 300 different tribes. Each Native American nation has its own history, culture, land base, and language. Broken treaties and harsh treatment forced by the white Europeans who settled America were what caused the decrease in their population. Historical documents confirm that native people were victims of numerous illegal and inhumane acts, and many issues — broken treaties, land claims, and quality education — still need to be addressed.[11]

How educators perceive their students does matter. It affects not only their academic performance and achievement, but also how the students think about themselves.

Regardless of previous prejudices or partiality, the current question in education concerns what can be done to teach effectively and successfully an increasingly diverse student population. Implementation must emanate from the teachers and administrators at the local school, for these are the educators who interact with the various students and are a major factor in their educational successes and failures. If a school has practices that prevent minority students from being part of a strong academic program, those practices will thwart academic success and limit minority students' opportunities for postsecondary education. An illustration would be a school or school system that offers advanced or accelerated classes but, because of biased policies, denies qualified minorities access to such classes. In the past such biased policies have ranged from using culturally unfair tests to holding the accelerated classes at locations inconvenient to a district's minority students.[12]

Valuing Every Student

Educators should value each and every student, treat every student without bias, and set high expectations for all students. Valuing students and imparting unbiased treatment will help build within the classroom an atmosphere of trust. Numerous students have lived in an environment in which there is suspicion and distrust of established, government-based institutions, such as the courts, the police, and the schools. Often this distrust is well founded. Teachers who model impartial behavior build bridges of trust and, as a result, garner increased cooperation and communication. Students who are comfortable and secure will more openly express their thoughts, feelings, ideas, knowledge, and opinions.[13]

Within this atmosphere of trust, there should be a recognition that high-quality work is expected from all. If teachers have low expectations from certain groups of students, they often receive what they expect. The opposite is equally true. When superior work is required and expected, it generally is received. Teachers should be prepared to teach and present courses that are challenging and interesting. Before students have completed elementary school, they should display competency in the basic skills of reading, writing, mathematics, and problem-solving and be exposed to the arts. By providing a strong education base to all students, teachers will build the foundation that students need for subsequent education and full citizenship.

In addition to the teacher building an atmosphere of trust and high expectations, the curriculum content and materials must be historically accurate and portray all groups authentically to correct previous ethnic stereotypes and misconceptions. The content should not be integrated into the curriculum in a superficial way. It requires more than a black history month, a women's awareness week, or a minority appreciation day to integrate meaningfully groups such as Native Americans, the disabled, and African Americans into the core curriculum. Although there is nothing wrong with using these strategies to help incorporate multicultural teaching, they should be only a small part of a truly comprehensive program. Incorporating a diverse curriculum requires that all subject matter be examined from the experiences and perspectives of many cultural viewpoints. Numerous ethnic groups have played a meaningful role in all disciplines, and so teaching about these contributions should be consistent, natural, and integrated.

Educators should carefully examine their curriculum materials to ensure that the inclusion of multicultural materials does not inadvertently promote cultural stereotypes. For example, a primary art class that has an activity of making headbands, clay beads, or sand paintings could easily present a distorted image of Native Americans. The same could be said of a music class that has a unit about Negro spirituals to experience the African-American culture. Although these activities do illustrate part of a history, if they do not present a complete picture and the whole essence of a culture, then they are introducing fundamental inaccuracies and inadvertent stereotyping. The best method for educators to determine if the curriculum accurately presents a particular gender, ethnicity, or race is to ask members of that group to help evaluate and revise the curriculum.[14]

Another caution when presenting a multicultural curriculum is not to eliminate the contributions of the dominant culture. One example that is frequently observed occurs at school Christmas or winter holiday programs. Presentations may honor the traditions of Hanukkah, Kwanzaa, Ramadan, and secular aspects of the holiday season, omitting entirely any presentation honoring the Christian religious aspect of Christmas. This is an egregious form of "over-correction." If educators are to be truly multicultural, *all* groups need to be authentically and accurately represented, including the majority one. If the influence and contributions of Christianity and Western European philosophy are ignored, the curriculum is equally historically dishonest.

Finding Strategies that Increase Learning

The increased diversity of students in the classroom has increased the diversity of preferred ways of learning. This statement should not be interpreted to mean that for each ethnic group there corresponds a specific, favored learning style. This type of one-to-one correlation does not exist. What does exist is a relationship between the culture in which students live and a culturally grounded learning preference. However, distinctions among the individuals within a group are as common as their similarities. Consequently, teachers need to be mindful and not expect all students in an ethnic group to respond in a similar manner to any particular learning style.[15]

For many years educators have used various instructional approaches. The challenge is to discover the ones that promote learning with each student. One solution is for teachers to become familiar with education research regarding instruction and the curriculum. For example, research conducted in the 1990s indicated that instruction that encouraged interaction and communication between the student and teacher advanced learning more than a directed lecture.[16] Another example: When limited-English-proficient students are part of the class, the core curriculum should be meaning-based, rather than grammar-based; contextual clues should be relevant to the students' backgrounds; and a bilingual approach should be employed.[17] Education journal articles concerning instructional approaches provide numerous potential techniques, but the most effective approaches are those that take the individual learner's learning characteristics into account, the one that works with each individual student.

As educators endeavor to improve the learning of minority students, all topics and outcomes require examination. Issues should not be avoided just because they are troublesome or controversial. An example would be the results of a study by the National Task Force on Minority High Achievement, formed in 1997 by the College Board. The study indicated that all things being seemingly equal, black students do not perform as well as white students. The purpose of the task force study was to monitor the achievement of students in middle-class, racially integrated communities to learn more about the academic disparity between black and white students and how the differences could be eliminated.[18]

In one of the communities — Evanston, Illinois — educators continually found black students from stable, educated, middle-class families who were earning low grades, despite having what was described as all the ingredients for academic success. These were not students from impoverished single-parent homes, but from homes with two parents who had college degrees and access to computers and tutors. To the credit of the educators in Evanston, the minority community did not become defensive or upset but brought the issue to the public square to find answers. Some reasons discussed included lingering racial inferiority complexes, low teacher expectations, an inadequate curriculum, lack of parental involvement, poor access to information, vestiges of racism in school, and peer pressure. High-achieving black students emphasized the problem of peer pressure by stating how they often were called "Oreos" for attaining high grades. Because high grades have been associated with white students, the black students who were in honors classes were asked if they were going to "be black" or going to achieve and "be white." No educator has all the answers, but these topics must be discussed if educators are going to meet the needs of all students.

No universal instructional approach will address the needs of all students. Teachers should use a variety of classroom strategies to help every student gain access to a quality curriculum. It is the amount of learning, not the mode of instruction, that is the most important variable. During the 1990s there was an education debate regarding whether it was more effective to teach reading by using phonics or a whole language approach. The debate became so political that some people associated phonics with the conservative movement and whole language was considered liberal. From a pedagogical viewpoint, some students learned to read more effectively when phonics was emphasized and others when a whole language approach was used. If a class of students requires both approaches in order to learn well, why not use both — or other effective methods?[19] Provide the students with extra help or tutoring when needed, so that failure never becomes a habit. After all, increasing the amount of learning, not promoting a mode of instruction, is the goal of education.

Reorienting Teacher Education

As classrooms become increasingly diverse, teacher education programs have the responsibility to prepare future teachers to address culture and learning styles. School systems have the same obligation toward teachers already working in the classroom. Unfortunately, numerous teacher education programs do not adequately explore the topic or prepare the preservice teacher for the diverse classroom. And when school systems sponsor multicultural education inservice training, the teachers characterize the instruction as not very useful. The preparation often consists of one-time workshops that seldom have follow-up or reinforcement sessions to help teachers *use* the new information in the classroom.

An example of an issue that should be addressed in preservice or inservice training is how teachers grounded in their own culture and teaching styles can successfully teach students from other cultures. Culture is involved in shaping learning styles, and teachers teach as they have been taught to learn. Students who share the teacher's ethnic background have an advantage, but other students often are adversely affected when the teacher is not adequately trained to use a variety of learning styles. The unfortunate aspect of inadequate training about instructional approaches is that some students are harmed. When teachers are well trained, studies indicate that student learning is not influenced by the race or ethnicity of the teacher and there appears to be no connection between the ethnic background of the teacher and student and student achievement.

All teachers are responsible for the teaching of all students — and all teachers should be sufficiently prepared to fulfill their responsibility.

Problems of "Resegregation" and Standardized Testing

The perception that many students are receiving an inferior education because of unresolved multicultural issues has prompted some choices that are causing a reemergence of segregation in the schools. Until the 1950s, legally there were separate and supposedly equal schools for whites and African Americans in the United States. However, the schools for black students were mostly underfunded and often received the throwaways from the schools for whites. In 1954 the U.S. Supreme Court declared separate schools inherently unequal and unconstitutional, but there was not meaningful desegregation until the 1970s. There was great hope in the minority community that their children would now have access to a high-quality education.[20]

During the 1990s many African-American parents complained that school desegregation did not produce the desired results; and in some cases, the parents claimed that the quality of education for black children was higher when the schools were segregated. Thus there have been some movements toward "resegregation."

In actuality, many schools were desegregated in name only. When students from different ethnic groups were assigned to the same school, they often were segregated within the school through tracking or ability grouping. Some parents of white students even lobbied for advanced academic programs in the school and then developed policies to prevent qualified minorities from having access. Thus so-called desegregated schools were soon segregated within by race, class, and ethnic group.

School systems also promoted segregation in the name of neighborhood schools. This practice was so prevalent that by 1991 the proportion of African-Americans attending predominantly minority schools was at the level of the early 1970s. Although minority parents would attempt to address these issues with the local school system, their voices often were ignored. Minority parents who had the resources sometimes believed their only recourse was to send their child to a private or charter school or to teach them at home.[21]

Members of minority communities also are concerned about the expanding use of standardized tests for making education decisions about their children. These tests are called "standardized" because they presumably are administered to all test takers using uniform directions and similar testing conditions, and then they are interpreted using norms that accurately measure such variables as knowledge, intelligence, and the skills or aptitudes of an individual or group. After being interpreted, a test's numerical score often is used to classify and evaluate test takers and so to justify school decisions regarding program admission criteria, ability tracking, placement in special classes, and graduation requirements. The current movement toward education standards, which began in the 1990s, has caused these tests to have an increasingly significant effect on education and a major influence on what students are taught.[22]

The major concern in the minority community regarding standardized tests is whether the results are valid or biased against minority students. The argument states that when testing students from various backgrounds, the probability of invalid results greatly increases as a result of cultural differences in experiential background, attitudes toward testing, and language. Because of these and other ethnic differences, the testing requirement of obtaining accurate and appropriate scores for all groups of students that are tested is unattainable. The test will be biased against some groups, and it usually is the minority community that is the victim of the bias. Because standardized tests are used to make education decisions and often are also used as a mechanism of social control, these biased tests are viewed as unjust by the minority community. Minority students are categorized as having lower achievement, aptitude, ability, and intelligence and unjustly placed in lower-level courses or denied access to accelerated programs.[23]

Court decisions from the 1960s to the present have partially upheld the argument that many standardized tests are biased against minority groups. In *Hobson* v. *Hansen* (1967), the court ruled that IQ tests used for tracking students were culturally biased because they were standardized using a white, middle-class sample and were not accurate for lower-class or black students. On appeal, other forms of ability grouping were allowed, but the use of racially discriminatory tests was prohibited. In a 1972 case, *Larry P.* v. *Riles*, the school system was using IQ tests to place students in EMR (educably mentally retarded) classes that resulted in a racial imbalance. Test validity became an important issue during the original trial and later appeals. The court set the following standards for validity: The same pattern of scores must appear for each subgroup, the mean score should be the same for different subgroups, and the results should correlate with other relevant criteria. Although experts argued that these standards were not psychometrically sound, the court ruled that the racial differences in test scores were caused by the test being culturally biased.

Language bias in IQ tests used to place students in special education classes was the issue in *Diana* v. *California State Board of Education* (1970). Although the case never came to trial, the state of California signed a consent decree that allowed nonwhite students to respond in their native language or English, banned the use of the test's verbal section, and directed the development of an IQ test appropriate for Mexican Americans and other students whose first language was not English. The Mexican-American students gained 15 points on the IQ test when allowed to respond in Spanish. And in the early 1970s the California state legislature passed a law requiring schools to substantiate IQ scores used for placement with the student's developmental history, cultural background, and academic achievement.

Since these court cases, educators have attempted to construct standardized tests that generate valid results. All educators are in agreement that if the tests being used are technically biased, they should be changed. The concern remains, however, whether the more recently developed standardized tests are free of bias and will not be harmful to minorities.

As debates regarding test bias continue, the use of standardized tests continues to extend. One extension that has produced considerable discussion is using standardized tests for measuring teacher competency. Opponents argue that teacher competency should be based on a performance test, not a standardized test, and suggest that such tests as the National Teacher Examination are biased against minorities. The proponents respond that the courts have ruled that the National Teacher Examination is valid for competency testing because the scores indicate presence or absence of knowledge. In addition, an Educational Testing Service validity study indicated that the National Teacher Examination was in compliance with the Civil Rights Act of 1964.[24]

Regardless of the outcomes of these debates, tests that produce invalid results harm the individuals being tested. Students may be denied opportunities, such as access to advanced levels of instruction, and placed in programs that are too easy or boring. In addition, low scores may harm self-esteem and confidence or lead to allegations that the student is lazy, not interested in school, or not intelligent. There have been cases where capable students quit school after receiving unfair and inaccurate test scores. It also should be remembered that even valid tests are not perfectly reliable. Even when performance on a test accurately and consistently measures a group or individual's performance on some real-world criteria, there are still some individuals who over- or under-perform. No test should be the sole criterion for making education decisions about programs or individuals. The chance of error, especially against minority students, is too great.

As the population of the United States enters the 21st century and becomes increasingly diverse, its citizens have the unique occasion to create an equitable multicultural and multi-ethnic society. Currently, more than a hundred different language groups and students from many more national and cultural groups are in American classrooms. According to demographic projections, by the middle of this new century there will be no single ethnic majority in the schools.

Every one of these students should be accepted and provided with a quality education. They not only require the skills to be productive, but they also need to accept, understand, and relate to each other. When educators become role models who authentically value diversity, then schools will be able to prepare their students for their roles in the diverse society of the 21st century.

Notes

1. San Diego County Office of Education, "Notes From Research, Diversity in the Classroom, 1997." www.sdcoe.k12.ca.us/notes/9/diverse.html

2. J.H. Wilkinson, *From* Brown *to* Bakke: *The Supreme Court and School Integration: 1954-1978* (Oxford: Oxford University Press, 1979).

3. D. Atkinson, G. Marten, and D.W. Sue, *Counseling American Minorities: A Cross-Cultural Perspective* (Dubuque: Wm. C. Brown, 1979).

4. E.H. Clarke, *Sex in Education: A Fair Chance for Girls* (Boston: James R. Osgood and Company, 1874).

5. National Center for Education Statistics, *The Condition of Education, 1998* (Washington, D.C.: U.S. Department of Education, 1998). nces.ed.gov/pubs/ce/index.html

6. U.S. Department of Health and Human Services, *Child Maltreatment 1997: Reports from the States to the National Child Abuse and Neglect Data System* (Washington, D.C.: U.S. Government Printing Office, 1999).

7. National Education Goals Panel, *National Education Goals Report: Building a Nation of Learners* (Washington, D.C., 1998). www.negp.gov

8. National Center for Education Statistics, *The Condition of Education in 1999* (Washington, D.C.: Department of Education, 1999). nces.ed.gov/pubs99/condition99/

9. San Diego County Office of Education, *Diversity in the Classroom, Notes from Research* (San Diego, 1997). www.sdcoe.k12.ca.us/notes/diverse.html

10. Ibid.

11. Ibid.

12. "Legal Issues in Testing," *Eric Digest* (1985). ERIC No. ED289884.

13. L. Cuban, *How Teachers Taught: Consistency and Change in American Classrooms, 1880-1990* (New York: Longman, 1993).

14. Howard Eugene Taylor, "Practical Suggestions for Teaching Global Education," *ERIC Digest* (June 1996): 1-4. ERIC No. ED395924.

15. Lorraine Monroe, *Nothing's Impossible* (New York: Time Books, 1997).

16. Donna E. Walker, *Strategies for Teaching Differently: On the Block or Not* (Thousand Oaks, Calif.: Corwin, 1998).

17. Tom Bello, "Improving ESL Learners' Writing Skills," *ERIC Digest* (1997): 1-4. ERIC No. ED409746

18. National Task Force on Minority High Achievement, *Reaching the Top* (New York: College Board, 1999).
19. Marlow Ediger, "How Should Reading Be Taught? A Public Forum Debate" (1995). Eric No. ED380791.
20. J.H. Wilkinson, *From* Brown *to* Bakke*: The Supreme Court and School Integration, 1954-1978* (Oxford: Oxford University Press, 1979).
21. Kathleen Manzo, "Report on School Segregation Comes as No Surprise to Many," *Black Issues in Higher Education* 10 (30 December 1993): 10-12.
22. Thomas R. Guskey, "Making the Grade: What Benefits Students," *Educational Leadership* 52 (October 1994): 14-20.
23. Theodore Cross, ed. "Explaining the Gap in Black-White Scores on IQ and College Admission Tests," *Journal of Blacks in Higher Education* 18 (Winter 1997-1998): 94-97.
24. "Legal Issues in Testing," *Eric Digest* (1985). ERIC No. ED289884.

Chapter 6

Ideology, Politics, and Education

From the formation of the United States until the latter part of the 20th century, the dominance of power remained with men who were white and Protestant. They determined the political, social, and educational directions of the country, and other groups had little input. In Article I of the Constitution of the United States, Indians were not even enumerated when determining the number of state representatives, and slaves were counted as three-fifths of a person. These people, along with free women, were not permitted to vote. It was not until 1870 and the ratification of the 15th Amendment that the right of male citizens to vote could not be denied because of race, color, or previous condition of servitude. The right to vote for women did not occur until 1920 with the ratification of the 19th Amendment.

Even with revisions in the Constitution, change did not occur quickly in society. Political leaders, in order to maintain power and control, prevented ethnic minorities from voting through the use of poll taxes, literacy tests, and violence. Often there were challenges in the courts, but it was not until the Civil Rights movement of the 1960s and 1970s that minorities who were previously disenfranchised began to gain genuine political power. The road to political power for women took a similar path.

Although white women were not prevented from voting after the passage of the 19th Amendment, they often voted as they were told by their husbands. And few women were elected to political office. In the 1960s and 1970s, during the time of the Civil Rights movement, the Women's Rights movement became a catalyst that placed an increasing number of females in powerful political and social roles.

Decisions regarding the education system of American society generally were intended to reinforce and perpetuate the dominant political power structure of the time. Despite such leaders as Thomas Jefferson and Horace Mann who argued that a democracy required a common school for the great mass of people in order to create an independent, free, and literate citizenry, most public schools defined this future citizenry as white male children. The future leaders that were to emerge from the public schools were not ethnic minorities or females. Although Jefferson wrote that the schools would be places where every talent could excel and would provide a foundation for a truly republican form of government, the schools actually bred a new type of aristocracy similar to that which Jefferson desired to eradicate.[1]

Realizing the Dream

The dream of universal education remained, and over the decades education in the United States became more universal and more equal for all. Although there have been many political and legal battles and it has taken some 200 years, the ideal of equal educational opportunity in the United States finally seems possible. Today's students are not prevented from attending a public school because of ethnic background or gender. When women enter college, they can major in any discipline and are not advised to enroll in the traditional "female" specialties of teaching or nursing. The number of females enrolled in higher education has increased to such a level that, in this new century, the number of women will exceed the number of men attending American colleges and universities.[2]

ntly, effective and universal schooling has become more
uential than at any previous time. Citizens require a strong
ion not only for the political reasons stated by Jefferson,
so to succeed economically and socially. Because education
such vital socioeconomic implications, sociologists use the
pression "intellectual capital" to describe the concept.[3] Intellec-
al capital has been directly related to a country's competitive-
ess and prosperity in the global environment and to individual
success in the local setting. For example, an educated person is
more likely to acquire more abilities, wealth, and status than a
person lacking in knowledge. However, the economic gap is not
the only consequence when there is not equal opportunity and
justice in the education arena. When the prospect to increase
one's intellectual capital is affirmed or denied, the outcome deter-
mines social class, school success or failure, and even psychological and physical health.

The importance of education and increasing one's intellectual
capital in the 21st century is so critical that educators have a moral
obligation to give all students the relevant experiences that they
require. This is especially true for younger students. When children
first enter school, some have already acquired intellectual capital
from the home and other pre-school experiences. These students
are able to use their knowledge to gain new knowledge and then
use this higher level of intellectual capital to gain even more
knowledge. However, other students enter school with limited
intellectual capital and lack the relevant experience and vocabulary.
In the classroom, these students have difficulty acquiring more
knowledge and often fall further and further behind. Failure to perform results in a loss of motivation to learn, and the lack of intellectual stimulation also lowers IQ. The gap in intellectual capital
continues to widen and, in the majority of cases, continues into
adulthood and becomes permanent. When educators are able to
better distribute intellectual capital in the early grades, they will
eliminate one major source of social injustice.

Because a high percentage of children entering school with
limited intellectual capital are minority students, the gap in intel-

lectual capital has acquired racial and ethnic implications. Explanations generally mention cultural and economic differences. For example, families from various ethnic backgrounds may provide their children with rich cultural experiences, but these experiences might not fully prepare their children for the American school system. A child's experience may enable the student to speak their parents' native language and English; but, when entering school, a limited vocabulary in English may cause performance to be at a lower level than what would have been achieved given the student's actual ability. Other examples of cultural differences that may provide intellectual capital — but not the kind required for school — include knowledge of a history or religion that is different from that learned by the majority.

Economic factors also determine how much intellectual capital a child accumulates before entering school. There is a direct relationship between the amount of intellectual capital and the number of diverse experiences a child encounters. A high proportion of poor families are ethnic minorities whose families cannot afford to provide their children with educational experiences. They may not be able to buy children's books for the home, visit museums, travel, use home computers, or provide other educational activities. Because of work schedules, the parents — or often, a single parent — in a low-income family might not be able to spend enough time with the child and offer the needed knowledge. Regardless of the reason, when students enter school with limited intellectual capital, educators have the responsibility to provide an environment where all students can build on their current intellectual capital and acquire more.[4]

Is Tracking the Answer?

This task of enriching students' intellectual capital is neither simple nor free of external pressure. Many times parents or politicians attempt to create an educational atmosphere in which certain groups of students will be able to maximize their intellectual capital, but too often this is done at the expense of other students.

Pressure of this sort sometimes influences educators to make decisions based on misconceptions or poor pedagogy. An illustration is schools placing students in "tracks," or set schedules of classes based on performance or hypothesized ability. In a simple tracking situation, students are placed in either compensatory or remedial classes, average classes (the mainstream ability track), or accelerated classes (a gifted or college-bound track). The belief is that tracking will prevent the better students from becoming bored and the slower students from becoming frustrated. This view arises from a gut sense that most teachers teach to the "average" student, thereby failing to meet the learning needs of the "top" and the "bottom" students. In contrast, educators who oppose tracking believe that students learn from each other across all ability levels. If more-effective educators are assigned the higher-level tracks, as is often the case, then students placed in a remedial track seldom return to the mainstream. And, on top of this, students are mistracked because of biases such as those I discussed in a previous chapter.

The debate concerning whether tracking is advantageous or not will assuredly continue; however, injustice and unfairness definitely occur when tracking is misused. For instance, parents who hold the misconception that some ethnic minority groups have lower intelligence have caused certain schools to establish policies that practically ensure that minority students will not have access to accelerated classes. Such a policy, for example, might state that students in a program for the highly gifted must score above 135 on an IQ test. Because many IQ tests are biased against certain minorities, this type of requirement can limit the minority presence in the program. This policy also could give an advantage based on economic status: If a student did not attain the required score on the IQ test that is given at school, many school districts permit private testing and use those results. These retests are expensive, and many low-income families cannot afford them. To add to the injustice, there have been instances in which parents paid to have private testing firms report false test scores so that their child would qualify. The resulting inequity is that many qualified minority students are excluded from special programs that benefit talented students and thus are not able to maximize intellectual capital. In such situations, though the school may be diverse, its higher-level track will consist mainly of white, middle- and upper-class students.

At the same time, some educators have expressed concern that pressuring students into accelerated tracks can be detrimental. For many students, advanced classes do not enrich their education or enhance their lives. Forcing students to read in preschool, study algebra in the fifth grade, and earn college credit at age 15 does not make them smarter. It may, however, take time away from other experiences that will make them better — more well-rounded — adults. Often the parents who push their children to achieve from birth are concerned more about social status than about what is educationally sound. For example, some parents worry that their child will not be accepted into the "correct" pre-school. A more balanced view is that students require time to grow, mature, and enjoy being young. Free time during the summer with family, in a sport's program, or doing volunteer work can be as important as earning college credit. There are many ways in which a young person must grow and develop. School is only part of the experience. It has always been like this in the past, and there is no reason to believe it will be otherwise in the future, however "advanced" we become.

"Liberal" and "Vocational-Technical" Education

Stratification also occurs within the curriculum based on the student's interests and intended profession. In broad terms, the curriculum may be divided into liberal education and vocational-technical education. Liberal education traditionally has been perceived as the course of study for students who have the intellectual capital to enter college, work in executive- or managerial-level positions, and become leaders in their community. The goals of these courses include developing responsible citizens, preparing leaders for the professions, and instilling in the students an increasing desire for knowledge — in other words, encouraging lifelong learning. In contrast, vocational and technical courses originally were designed to prepare students with lower intellectual capital for vocational or trade jobs that did not require college degrees. These included the building trades, secretarial positions, some health-care careers, and other occupations the student will enter after leaving high school.

The differences between liberal and vocational-technical education has diminished since the establishment of the first vocational-technical career academy programs in the 1960s. Today vocational programs no longer are considered the domain for those with low intellectual capital. Instead of entering the labor market directly from high school, most career-oriented programs require at least two years of postsecondary education if the student expects to be academically and technically proficient in a field. Vocational high school programs now include studies in environmental technology, computer engineering, applied electrical science, avionics, aviation technology, and other highly complex subjects. Students who are part of a vocational or technical program often earn an undergraduate and even a graduate college degree in their discipline.[5]

The environment of the 21st century requires that all students receive the benefits of both a liberal and a vocational-technical education. Every student should have the knowledge to control his or her own life by making informed and responsible choices, not just vocationally, but as citizens and human beings. In the past, liberal education in the United States focused on the history of America, its institutions, and the central ideas that have shaped its culture. The current environment requires that students study not only the traditional ideas of American culture, but also the ideas and beliefs of other cultures. Comprehension must extend beyond the local environment so that students can participate successfully in the international political and cultural arena of an ever-changing global marketplace. This requires proficiency in current technology and fluency in English, at least one foreign language, mathematical reasoning, and the sciences. By providing a comprehensive liberal education program, educators will be able to demonstrate how disciplines and perspectives are interrelated and provide students with a shared sense of time and culture.

Liberal education also requires a connection between general knowledge and a major field of study. Although people do not live in order to work, they work in order to live and must have a career. Teachers of both liberal and vocational education courses should integrate their curricula so that academic coursework is directly related to the vocation sequence and the structure provides for a smooth transition from school to work. Models that have proven successful include thematic learning, partnerships with business, mentoring programs, and structured out-of-school learning experiences. By providing a carefully structured program, educators will endow students with technical *and* academic knowledge and the desire for lifelong learning essential in a rapidly changing workplace.

Organizations Weigh In

In addition to deciding the best methods for students to acquire knowledge and increase their intellectual capital, educators also must decide what learning is meaningful and should be part of the curriculum. There are numerous professional, political, social, health, religious, education, and other types of organizations, all trying to influence what is taught in schools. The main function of some of the associations is to improve education, and these are considered by most teachers to be an integral part of the education community. Three examples (among many) are the National Council of Teachers of Mathematics, Phi Delta Kappa International, and the American Alliance for Health, Physical Education, Recreation, and Dance. As part of their function, these organizations and their counterparts publish education journals, sponsor conferences, fund research, and provide information to help educators develop strong curricula. For example, the National Council of Teachers of Mathematics has deeply influenced the current curriculum in mathematics by publishing curriculum standards for each grade level and recommending how to integrate technology in the classroom.[6]

Other organizations are less directly involved in education but publish curricula that support the group's goals and agenda. Frequently, the suggested curricula are quite different. An example would be two groups concerned about the high teenage pregnancy rate and the transmission of sexual diseases. One group, the Family Research Council, is convinced that a solution to the problem is a school program that promotes abstinence until marriage. The other group, Planned Parenthood, believes that teenagers will engage in sexual relations regardless of the curriculum and the solution is to promote safe sex. Both organizations develop or support school lessons based on their convictions and then attempt to persuade school systems to adopt their program.

Another example is the debate in the science program regarding the teaching of evolution and creationism. In 1925 the debate over human origins received notable attention in the United States when John Scopes was charged with violating a Tennessee law forbidding the teaching of evolution. Scopes was found guilty, but his conviction was overturned by the Tennessee state supreme court. However, the court upheld the statute regarding evolution. It was not until 1968 that the U.S. Supreme Court declared that states could not forbid the teaching of evolution, and teaching creationism as a science was almost abolished in the public schools. Currently there is a renewed attempt by theistic groups to incorporate creationism into the school curriculum. Most in the current movement claim that they are not trying to remove evolution from the public schools; they simply desire the creationist view to be presented. These groups have written books and course units that, according to their adherents, present scientific and rational reasons that support a creationist view of the universe. Critics claim that the creationist curriculum is not science, but only religion claiming to be science.[7]

Interest groups often put a good deal of pressure on school systems, especially when the issue has a strong ideological foundation. A group's ideology or worldview forms the basis for decisions in all areas of life. Using the previous example, people who believe in the literal truth of the Genesis account of creation will resolutely believe that this truth must be taught in school. They often petition schools and school boards to incorporate creationism into the curriculum, and in many towns and cities they stand for election to the local school board when their requests are denied. Of course, people who strongly support a different worldview petition just as strongly for their position. These forms of action also are true of the debates regarding sex education, drug and alcohol policies, and many other philosophical and moral issues.

Debates Include Modes of Instruction

In addition to determining what should be taught, ideology also influences beliefs about how the classroom should be structured. People who believe that there are universal scientific or moral truths waiting to be discovered assert that the class should be directed by a teacher who will introduce students to these truths. Without a learned teacher directing the instruction, students might easily believe error to be truth and render incorrect conclusions about their world. Others contend that these declared truths are not universal, but only a part of Western ideology and culture. Instead of casting students into a circumscribed cultural mold, schools should strive for diversity, equality, and tolerance of ideas. Instead of being the all-knowing leader, the teacher should function as a guide in the construction of knowledge. Students are not to be just recipients of knowledge, but also involved in social interaction, individual exploration, and creativity. The classroom will then be a place where all have a voice, where all voices are valued and everyone learns from one another.[8]

This debate is another example of politics or ideology inciting people to fervently defend one side or the other of an issue and to attack the other side. It is possible, of course, for both views to be pedagogically sound, depending on the subject, the project, the type of student, and other factors. Few would disagree that classrooms should have a learned teacher guiding the instruction. If all that was necessary was a person to facilitate student-centered discussion, an instructor certified to teach the discipline would not be required. Nevertheless, the teacher, regardless of competence, is not an all-knowing oracle, and the students are more than passive recipients of information. Therefore, in addition to acquiring knowledge from teacher-guided instruction, students should be guided into purposeful individual exploration and creativity that corresponds to the discipline being taught. The answer, in fact, is balance.

Another example of an intense debate regarding mode of instruction involves the use of Ebonics or African American Vernacular English (AAVE) in the curriculum. On 18 December 1996 the Oakland Unified School District Board of Education approved a policy that affirmed the need to develop Standard American English for all students and stated that all effective instructional strategies should be used to ensure that all students are proficient in English. Since 53% of the students in the Oakland schools were African American, the school district believed that the language development of these students would be enhanced by recognizing and understanding the language structures of Ebonics and that teachers should be trained to use Ebonics in the classroom. The proponents of this plan emphasized that Ebonics is a separate language and that students could learn standard English more easily if they were taught in Ebonics. Criticism came quickly. Many critics argued that Ebonics is not a separate language and that it made no sense to teach standard English by using incorrect English. They argued that the actual purpose for declaring Ebonics to be a language was to qualify for federal funds that were earmarked for bilingual programs. The controversy made national news.[9]

Concerns About Violence

At this juncture in American education, the problem of rising school violence seems to be a major threat to effective teaching and learning. School violence is not a recent phenomenon. In the 1950s the problem was called juvenile delinquency, and disagreements were often settled with a fist fight. Today, not only has the number of antisocial behaviors increased, but there also is a high probability that school violence will involve a weapon, especially a gun. The public concern over school violence in the 1990s prompted Congress to include a goal in the Educate America Act that states, "By the year 2000, every school in America will be free of drugs and violence and will offer a disciplined environment conducive to learning."[10]

This goal, like most of the others in that legislation, was not reached by the turn of the century; educators still are seeking long-term solutions. The factors that contribute to school violence are diverse and complex. These include inadequate parenting practices, such as lack of supervision at home, lack of family involvement with school, and overexposure of children to television, movie, and videogame violence. In increasing numbers, parents are working outside the home and are not available for consultation with school officials when problems occur. Sometimes parents simply refuse to work with the school, or they believe that it is the school's fault that their child is having discipline problems. There are even a few parents who tell their children that they do not have to obey their teacher and that fighting is a legitimate way to solve problems.[11]

Other factors that contribute to school violence include peer pressure, drugs and alcohol, and bias. Peer pressure is most likely the fastest growing reason for violence in the schools. When students do not feel a part of their family, they often find acceptance in a peer group or gang. Members of neighborhood gangs frequently have a them-against-us mentality that erupts in acts of violence against each other, those in authority, or society in general. Drugs and alcohol also are involved in school violence. Their use is found in all geographic locations, levels of family income, and ethnic backgrounds and does not vary significantly across categories. In the 1990s, the "war on drugs" appeared to have some positive effects as the percentage of students in grades 6 through

12 who use heroin, cocaine, marijuana, and crack decreased. The use of alcohol, however, did not decline; and at this writing, alcohol is the number-one drug used by secondary school students.

One of the more disturbing trends regarding school violence is the increasing number of violent acts relating to racial or religious bias. As diversity in American society and schools continues to grow, increased tension among the various ethnic, religious, and political groups also occurs. For example, one ethnic group might blame another ethnic group for economic difficulties or perceived negative changes in culture. Religious and political groups will disagree over moral issues and what laws should be enforced. Over the last few years, there have been many discussions regarding laws relating to abortion, the death penalty, affirmative action, and various lifestyles. At times disagreements went beyond verbal exchanges and became violent. Homosexuals have been assaulted or killed because of their lifestyles and beliefs, abortion clinics have been bombed, and ethnic minorities have been assaulted or killed simply because they *are* minorities. Acts of violence such as these have continued to increase both on and off the school campus.[12]

When assessing school violence, most people believe that students are both the perpetrators and the victims. Although this often is the case, students are neither the only perpetrators nor the only victims. Teachers are targeted by students, particularly in urban areas. Victims often are the young, inexperienced, female teachers or teachers who are strict and insist on high academic and behavioral standards. The violence against teachers who insist on quality work and proper behavior often causes these teachers to lower standards — or to leave the profession altogether. This is especially true when the teacher believes that the school administration cannot provide a safe environment or the teacher does not receive support from school administrators. In addition, many teachers are concerned that if they intervene in student acts of violence, they will be sued or accused of child abuse.[13]

Teachers must intervene when a student is a victim of another student's unkind act. In 1977 the Supreme Court wrote in

Ingraham v. *Wright* that school administrators have "the duty of ensuring that the school environment is a safe one for students."[14] Centuries ago, the Hebrew prophet Isaiah warned Israel of negative consequences when justice is turned back and righteousness stands afar off. The same warning should be shouted in the schools, for many of the perpetrators of school shootings that have made headlines have been victims of teasing or worse. While this does not excuse the acts of violence, it should remind all educators that bullying should not be ignored. There are too many cases where educators ignore sexual harassment or name calling aimed at students because of their physical looks or sexual orientation, or where educators show preference to certain groups of students, such as star athletes, cheerleaders, or the children of community leaders. All students deserve equal rights and equal protection and a safe school. It is the responsibility of all educators to help provide that type of environment.

Educators have developed or implemented a variety of measures, with varying degrees of success, to ensure school safety. The most often used security measure is to have school staff and faculty monitor activities in and around the school. In some areas, schools hire off-duty police officers or security guards. Another measure that has been effective is employing parents as monitors or teacher aides. When parents from a neighborhood are visible at a school, students from that community are less likely to misbehave. Some other strategies have included dress codes, counseling and conflict resolution programs, classes in parenting skills, and extended school hours with organized activities. Although there is no consensus regarding the best way to address school violence, most strategies attempt to protect victims, instill better moral values, and render nonviolent conflict resolution.

A meaningful aspect of nonviolent conflict resolution is to instill within students the ability to discuss issues in a logical, non-caustic manner and to respect the rights of others. There will always be conflict and disagreement in any culture. When people disagree, persuasion should be verbal, not violent. One heartening aspect of the United States is its judicial tolerance of diversity and various points of view. The First Amendment to the Constitution guarantees freedom of speech and the right to peaceably assemble so that every voice has a right to be heard in the public square. Depending on the circumstances, the public square may be a classroom, a local government meeting, an Internet bulletin board, a letter to the newspaper, an e-mail to an elected official, or any other type of shared communication. Each person has the privilege, some say the obligation, to contribute to the public discourse and to help shape culture. Perhaps the most relevant aspect of education is to provide students with the skills to test and evaluate the ideas of others, to form their own worldviews, and to be able to present their views in a clear and coherent way.[15]

Notes

1. Eyler Robert Coates, "Thomas Jefferson on Politics & Government: Publicly Supported Education," in *The Writings of Thomas Jefferson*, edited by Albert Ellery Bergh and Andrew Adgate Lipscomb (Washington, D.C.: Thomas Jefferson Memorial Association of the United States, 1999). etext.lib.virginia.edu/jefferson/quotations/jeff1370.htm

2. Washington State Office of Financial Management, *Higher Education Enrollment Statistics and Projections: 1999-2001 Biennium*, Chapter 7 (Olympia, Wash., 1999). Eric No. ED430449.

3. John J. Patrick, *Education for Engagement in Civil Society and Government* (Bloomington, Ind.: ERIC Clearinghouse for Social Studies/Social Science Education, 1998). Eric No. ED423211.

4. Ron Renchler, "Poverty and Learning," *ERIC Digest* (May 1993): 1-3. Eric No. ED357433.

5. Office of Vocational and Adult Education, *Career Academy Programs* (Washington, D.C.: U.S. Department of Education, 1999).

6. National Council of Teachers of Mathematics, *Principles and Standards for School Mathematics* (Reston, Va., 2000).

7. J.P. Moreland and John Mark Reynolds, *Three Views on Creation and Evolution* (Grand Rapids, Mich.: Zondervan, 1998).

8. Marceline Thompson and Linda Pledger, "Cooperative Learning Versus Traditional Lecture Format: A Preliminary Study," paper presented at the Annual Meeting of the National Communication

Association, New York, 19-24 November 1998. ERIC No.
ED426418.

9. Steven Fox, "The Controversy over Ebonics," *Phi Delta Kappan* 79
(November 1997): 237-40.

10. Goals 2000: Educate America Act, Public Law 103-227 (108 Stat.
125).

11. National School Board Association, *Violence in the Schools* (Alexandria, Va., 1993).

12. Daniel J. Flannery, *School Violence: Risk, Preventive Intervention,
and Policy* (ERIC Clearinghouse on Urban Education, 1997).
http://eric-web.tc.columbia.edu/monographs/uds109

13. M.H. Futrell, "Violence in the Classroom: A Teacher's Perspective," in *Schools, Violence and Society*, edited by A.M. Hoffman
(New York: Greenwood, 1996).

14. 430 U.S. 651, 654.

15. W. DeJong, "School-Based Violence Prevention: From the Peaceable School to the Peaceable Neighborhood," *Forum: National Institute for Dispute Resolution* 25 (Spring 1994): 8-14.

Chapter 7

Economics and Education

Building an education environment that increases intellectual capital requires money. When there is insufficient funding, schools often lack required books, equipment, classrooms, and even faculty and staff. The result is classes that are too large, schools that are overcrowded, textbooks that are outdated, and science and computer labs without the needed equipment. As the United States approached the turn of the century, the number of public schools without adequate funds increased as federal, state, and local governments attempted to limit spending, better control their budgets, and limit tax increases. Money for public education was linked to specific outcomes as the public demanded that educators be more accountable. This continues to be true, especially at state and local levels of government, where spending on education is frequently a large percentage of the state, county, or city budget. In addition, constraints on public school funding also occur when locally elected officials are not favorably inclined toward public education.[1]

Private schools also require money to operate, but they are not influenced as much by the political climate and the whims of legislators as are the public schools. Instead of depending primarily on public tax money, the majority of private school budgets are funded by tuition fees, gifts, endowments, and sponsoring organizations. This means that their monetary base is influenced by the perceived reputation of the school. When a private school is highly regarded, parents who can afford the tuition are willing to send their children to the school. They also support the school by donating to school fund drives and other fundraising activities. However, most private schools are not completely free of public influence. It should be noted that most private schools do receive some public support, either directly or indirectly, by accepting public funds based on student enrollment, receiving tax benefits, or using the facilities and programs of local public schools.

In an attempt to lessen the effect of the political process on their programs, public schools have replicated the fundraising programs of the private schools. Public colleges, universities, and even some secondary schools, in fact, are not that much different from their private counterparts. Public colleges and universities charge students tuition, solicit funds from school alumni and friends, establish endowment programs, market their name for use on clothing, sell tickets and television rights to school sporting events, and engage in other fundraising activities. Although public secondary schools do not charge tuition, they do raise money through various activities, such as soliciting funds from parents and others, selling tickets to school sporting events, engaging in fund drives, and forming partnerships with businesses.

Winners and Losers in Funding

As schools compete for financial support from politicians and the public, financial winners and losers begin to emerge. The schools that are the financial victors can provide their students with up-to-date textbooks, the latest technology, a modern campus, and other educational benefits. Students who attend the poorer schools with insufficient funding become education's have-nots and experience inferior academic conditions. In certain areas, public schools that have major funding disparities can be found in the same city and only a few blocks apart. Although such disparities commonly involve inner-city schools, funding inequities also exist in rural and suburban neighborhoods. In fact, the problem of funding partiality presents itself in essentially every state. The education of some public school students is funded at several times the amount of other public school students, and adequacy of education opportunity functions almost solely on the basis of which school the student attends and where it is located.

One reason for funding inequity is that states have assigned control of school financing to local school districts. If the district is affluent and has high property values, then the district is able to fund the schools at a higher level with revenue generated from a relatively low tax rate. The opposite occurs in less-affluent districts. Districts with a low or declining tax base must finance their schools with low levels of receipts that are often generated from a comparatively high tax rate. For example, during the latter 1980s the wealthiest school district in Texas spent almost seven times the amount of money per student as the poorest district. A comparison of school districts in all 50 states indicates that the most prosperous school districts routinely spent two to five times more per student than the districts with the least wealth.[2]

Differences in per student expenditure also occur when comparing schools across the states and comparing schools by type of neighborhood. During the 1980s and 1990s, the average spent in the highest-spending state was approximately three times the amount expended by the lowest-spending state. Although some of the variance could be justified by the differences in the cost of providing an education, that factor did not explain all of the discrepancy. For example, Arkansas and Alaska spent approximately $2,500 and $7,500 per student, respectively, during the 1989-90 school year. Anyone who has been to the two states knows that the cost of living is higher in Alaska than in Arkansas, but not three times higher. In addition to differences by state, there are funding contrasts based on a school's community. Suburban schools in the 1990s spent about 10% more per student than did rural schools and 15% more per student than did urban schools.

Even within the same school district, funding inequities occur because citizens living in one section of a school district have more political power than people living in another part. The influence of these constituents can cause the per student funding of one or more schools in a district to exceed what others in the district would consider equitable. The schools that are better funded often have stronger academic programs, enhanced extracurricular activities, more up-to-date facilities, and more resources. Differences in education opportunities caused by school funding disparities often are heightened by family resources. Parents with the political power to control how tax money is spent often have a higher socioeconomic status than those who have less power, and thus they are able to direct funds to schools attended by their children or the children of their friends. In addition to receiving extra funds, when the better-funded school has a need, the parents of children who attend that school have the resources and the will to satisfy the request. The families of students at less-advantaged schools often are low in socioeconomic status and are not able to donate to their child's school. As a result, schools in poor neighborhoods accumulate burdens, receive lower public funding, and receive fewer gifts from parents

Funding and Technology

A 21st century example of the effects of school funding inequities can be seen in the unequal implementation of technology in schools. During the 1990s and into this century, educators recognized the growing importance of computer-based technology and the Internet. President Clinton, in his 1998 commencement address at MIT, echoed this belief when he stated, "Until every child has a computer in the classroom and the skills to use it, until every student can tap the enormous resources of the Internet, until every high-tech company can find skilled workers to fill its high-wage jobs, America will miss the full promise of the information age." Buying, installing, and implementing technology in the classrooms of America requires a high level of funding. Because of funding inequities, wealthy schools are more than two times more likely to have Internet access in the classroom than are poorer schools.[3]

This example also reveals the effects of the socioeconomic status of the school district and the student. When a school serves a wealthy attendance zone and requires more funds for technology, the parents often will donate funds or computer equipment. Schools in less-affluent areas serve mainly families that cannot afford to donate technology, and Internet access is not provided. Again, the wealthier schools are able to procure increased resources, and the gap between the haves and have-nots widens into what has been called the "digital divide" between rich and poor schools. The wealth of the home also has a major effect on the Internet resources available for the student. Students attending wealthier schools are more likely to have Internet access at school *and* at home. Parents of means buy their children computers and subscribe to an Internet service. Thus, even if the school does not provide Internet access, these students can learn Internet skills at home.

Inequity in school funding also has racial and ethnic components. Of the children who are identified as poor according to United States government guidelines, more than 80% are black or Hispanic. Not only are these families unable to afford educational resources for the home, these poor students often are clustered in schools that are visibly underfunded. This occurs at all levels. During 1998 in the University of North Carolina system, the predominantly white colleges received funding to provide their students with several state-of-the-art computer labs with Internet access available 24 hours per day. Students living in the dorms at these schools have access through a data line in their room. At the historically black universities in the same system, the funding of facilities for computers and Internet access was inadequate, and the majority of the computers designated for students were more than four years old. And at one historically black university in the system, Winston-Salem State University, the library had only four computers that were connected to the Internet and were accessible to all students. Fortunately, this example had a happy ending. Because of pressure on the governing bodies by students, faculty, and alumni, Winston-Salem received funds to upgrade its technology; and by 2001, the campus library and several departments had state of the art computer labs, and there was campuswide Internet access.

Apart from school, students of low socioeconomic status are more likely to live in an environment that limits their intellectual growth. The environmental dangers of poverty include lower birth weights, poorer nutrition, higher exposure to drugs and AIDS, and a higher probability of being injured than are found in more affluent environments. In the inner city, poor children are seven times more likely to be abused or neglected than are their wealthier peers. Any one of these variables would inhibit academic performance; and not surprisingly, as many as one million low-income students withdraw from school each year and do not earn a high school diploma. Failure to graduate perpetuates a cycle of poverty, for it is estimated that the income lost during one's lifetime as a result of not having a high school diploma is between $20,000 and $200,000 per individual. Cumulative personal income lost in the United States because of the dropout rate is enormous. For the class of 1981 alone, the total income lost by dropouts from high schools across the United States has been estimated at more than $235 billion and lost tax revenue at $68 billion. These numbers show why educators believe that for every dollar spent today keeping low-income students in school, U.S. taxpayers will save almost five dollars in future costs.[4]

Many states have incorporated funding plans to ensure that every school has the minimum funding required to provide all students with a basic level of education. Most of these "foundation" or "equalizing formula" plans have not accomplished their goal of eliminating funding inequities. In most cases, the wealthier school districts simply add their property tax revenue to the amount provided by the equalizing formula plan. The less-wealthy districts, though they might receive more basic-level funding, still do not have the local tax base to stay equal with the affluent districts. Another problem concerns the political definition of a basic level of education. In several states, there have been court cases that challenged state funding plans, saying that the plan violated either the education clause or the equal protection clause of a state's constitution. The courts have overturned several state funding plans but have not presented clear guidelines to remedy the financial disparities.

Federal Initiatives

The federal government also has attempted to provide funds through a variety of programs to help disadvantaged schools and poor students. One program, Head Start, is endeavoring to increase the preparedness of disadvantaged preschool children for their entry into the public schools. During the 1990s the evaluations of the Head Start programs were frequently positive as participants demonstrated short-term benefits. These included better health, improved cognitive and social development, and grade promotion. However, increases in such areas as IQ were small and dissipated within two years. For low-income students already in school, federal funds from the Title I program were made available to help state and local agencies establish compensatory classes in writing, mathematics, and reading. The various plans funded through Title I have received mixed reviews, but overall the achievement gap between poorer and richer students has narrowed only slightly.

Another way in which the federal government has provided resources for schools is to either encourage or require business and industry to furnish certain services to schools at a reduced cost. An example from the 1990s that still benefits schools is the amendment on universal service to the Telecommunications Act. Signed into law on 1 February 1996, one of the act's key objectives was to "expand and maintain an existing system of universal service that provides high-cost areas, low income families, and schools, libraries, and rural health care providers with affordable access to advanced telecommunications." One year after becoming law, the Federal Communications Commission ruled that all K-12 schools and libraries should receive up to $2.25 billion a year in discounts for telecommunication service.[5]

Discounts, called the E-rate, are determined on a sliding scale and range from 20% to 90%. Although the average discount is approximately 60%, the least-wealthy schools can receive 80% to 90% discounts. Internet access and internal connections also are discounted. The popularity of the E-rate became apparent during the initial application process, when more than 30,000 requests were submitted for more than $2 billion in discounts. In this initial process, 53% of the funds were requested by the poorest schools and libraries and less than 1% by the wealthier schools. But a problem for many low-income schools was that funds to purchase equipment for using the Internet were not available, because the E-rate did not include money for computers, software, or other peripherals.

Some educators have suggested that the primary difficulty is lack of federal money. Because federal funds usually represent less than 10% of a state education budget, there is rarely enough funding for required special programs; and thus only limited success can be expected unless federal funds are supplemented by state and local funding. In addition, there also have been allegations that Title I funds were misused and not spent for their intended purpose. One accusation asserted that in some states, Title I services were distributed throughout the school districts without attempting to target the intended (disadvantaged) student population.

Money by itself is not the solution to the problem — or any problem, for that matter. Many studies have revealed that increases in expenditures are not strongly correlated to improved student performance; and if money continues to be spent as it has been in the past, increases are unlikely to occur. This does not negate the importance of financial equity. But finances are only a piece of the puzzle. Research is required to determine what programs and strategies will produce increased learning so that increased funds can be spent wisely.

Competition for the Dollars

A reality of the late 20th century and into the 21st century has been the competition for limited dollars to fund expanding education needs. Starting in the 1980s, there was a social movement that questioned the effectiveness of public education and the amount of tax money being spent on funding the public schools. This social movement also questioned the legitimacy of federal deficit spending and the amount of money people paid in taxes. The movement proved quite successful. People in some states passed referenda that limited the taxing power of their state or county governments. At the federal level, a balanced budget was passed in the late 1990s for the first time in more than a generation, and the tax rate at state and county levels remained stable or fell slightly. However, the demands placed on public schools during this time were increasing. Schools were asked to support free or reduced-fee breakfast and lunch programs, bilingual education programs, special education programs, health programs, and other services. With all of these expectations, people should not be surprised that many school districts, especially the less affluent ones, currently do not have funds for maintaining their buildings, providing teachers or students with educational materials, or constructing new schools.[6]

Another significant sphere influenced by funding is the ability to recruit teachers. Increasingly, schools are competing for staff as a teacher shortage looms. Educators, like people in any profession, are attracted by higher rates of pay. In the teaching profession, this may be especially true because teacher salaries, on average, are below those in other professions that require an equivalent education. Several explanations have been presented for the low rate of teacher pay. One reason is simply that the states cannot afford to pay higher salaries to public school teachers, and the citizens of the state will not tolerate a higher tax rate. Another rationale is that for much of the 20th century, school teaching was performed by women who wished to work outside the home. The pay for these women in teaching — and those in other traditionally female-dominated careers, such as nursing — has been below pay for males in comparable jobs. By 2000, the pay in many traditionally female occupations was approaching parity with males in equivalent jobs; but unfortunately, this has not occurred in teaching. Currently, teaching is one of the lowest-paying jobs based on the level of education required.

Low pay has caused many talented people to reject the idea of going into teaching as a profession, especially in certain disciplines. The higher the salary in the discipline, the less likely a person interested in that discipline will choose to teach. One example is mathematics. In the secondary schools the shortage of mathematics teachers is so severe that some estimate that as many as half of all mathematics classes are taught by teachers who are certified in some other discipline. This has caused recruitment competition among school districts. The wealthier school districts recruit the best teacher candidates from schools of education and other school districts with the promise of higher pay and better working conditions. It should not be surprising that the majority of teachers prefer working in the more affluent schools. Thus the less-wealthy communities, in addition to having inferior education facilities, often have to hire educators that were not their first choice. During the 1990s the federal government proposed programs designed to attract teachers to less-affluent schools, but these programs had minimal effect.

Gambling for Education

A method employed by an increasing number of states to raise funds for education is to establish lotteries. In a lottery, the players risk a small amount of money against steep odds in the hope of winning a large prize; and the net proceeds go to a public good, such as education. It is clearly the most widespread form of gambling in the United States, with games operated in most every state and the District of Columbia. Lotteries have the worst odds of any common form of gambling; but they have the highest potential payoff, often amounting to millions of dollars. For the states with lotteries, the profit rate (sales minus payouts but not including costs) is approximately 38% of sales. State lotteries continue to be debated, but they became increasingly accepted during the 1990s.

Although most people think of lotteries as a recent phenomenon, lotteries were popular even in Colonial America. They were used in the 1600s to finance public projects, such as the building of streets, wharves, and churches. In the 1700s, buildings at

Harvard and Yale were financed using a lottery. Current state lotteries began in 1964 with the New Hampshire lottery.

The main reason presented for a state-run lottery is that it is a "painless" source of revenue, and supporters emphasize how profits from the lottery can be used to support the public good by increasing funds for popular causes or reducing the need to raise taxes. For example, in 1994 Georgia mandated that funds from its lottery be used for education projects not previously in existence. These included funding college scholarships, establishing prekindergarten classes, and purchasing technology for public school classrooms. In New Mexico a similar program was established, where 60% of the lottery funds went toward public school construction and 40% went toward college tuition assistance.[7]

Critics of the lottery are concerned about the desirability of gambling, the problem of compulsive gambling, its effect on lower-income groups, and effects on public policy in general. Lottery promoters aver that illegal gambling already exists and that a state lottery actually will suppress illegal gambling, plus the money wagered goes to the state instead of to the criminals. Critics counter that, regardless of any alleged benefits, lotteries expand the number of people who gamble, promote addictive behavior, and create a conflict between the state's desire to increase revenue and its duty to protect the public welfare. As an example, critics cite lottery advertisements aimed at low-income groups. One example was a billboard located in an impoverished Chicago neighborhood that promoted how a person can go from low-income housing on Washington Boulevard to Easy Street by playing the Illinois State Lottery.

Lottery critics also charge that the alleged beneficiaries of lottery profits often do not receive extra revenue. When a lottery provides extra funding for public education, the state legislature can simply reduce state appropriations by an identical amount and then spend the "saved" money on other projects. Lotteries thus increase the availability of discretionary funds but do not provide more for the designated recipients of lottery revenues. In Florida, for example, the state spent 60% of its budget on education before establishing a lottery with proceeds designated for education. Five years after the lottery was established, the share of the state's budget specified for education had declined to 51%. Studies indicate that other states also spent a greater portion of their budgets on education before they established lotteries and that education spending usually declined after a lottery was established. In Virginia, lottery officials actually publicly apologized in 1997 for implying that lottery proceeds for education were *in addition* to the legislature's funding.

Funding Tensions Continue

Whenever there is revenue to be distributed, whether from a lottery or any other source, there will be a variety of interest groups attempting to share in the proceeds. This causes tension among politicians, educators, and parents. Educators, along with others, battle for the maximum possible percentage of the total distribution. This occurs at every level of government. Although public money is designated for the public good, people disagree over what constitutes the public good and the amounts of money that should be allocated to different causes. The effort to obtain adequate funds does not end when the government agency designates the allocation for education. Within the various education categories, there are conflicts over the amount each group deserves. Some education institutions even hire lobbyists to increase a school's chances for more funding.

Parents are involved in the struggle for increased funding at all levels, but they are especially vocal at the local level. Most parents desire the best education possible for their children, and so it is not surprising that most parents are self-serving and request funding for the programs that directly concern their child. For example, when a parent has a student involved in an academically gifted program, that parent often will lobby to be sure that the academically gifted program is amply funded. Lobbying requests include not only the academic programs but other school-related activities, such as sports, clubs, and social programs.

As I stated previously, the parents who experience the most success lobbying for funds are those of higher socioeconomic status. These people often enjoy power of position or power of influence and are able to access funds for education programs that directly benefit their children. Frequently this indicates that there will be inadequate funding for programs available to students from less-wealthy families. It is at this juncture that politicians, educators, and parents should move beyond any narrow agenda and determine what is truly the "public good" regarding current education programs. If educators are to provide resources for *all* students and produce an educated citizenry, funding should not be based on political power but on educational need. This will require educators and education organizations to continue their efforts to develop a challenging and rigorous curriculum for all students, provide extra help when required, support high-quality research, educate the public, and work to obtain funding for worthwhile programs.

Notes

1. Jonathan Kozol, *Savage Inequalities: Children in American Schools* (New York: Crown, 1991). William Cooley and Debra Pomponio, "The Financial Equity Debate," *Pennsylvania Educational Policy Studies Number 15* (Springfield, Va.: ERIC, 1993). ERIC No. ED355665.
2. Ron Renchler, *Financial Equity in the Schools* (Eugene, Ore.: ERIC Clearinghouse on Educational Management, December 1992). ERIC No. ED350717.
3. Office of Educational Technology, *Discounted Telecommunications Services for Schools and Libraries: E-Rate Fact Sheet* (Washington, D.C.: U.S. Department of Education, 1998). http://www.ed.gov/technology/comm-mit.html
4. Ron Renchler, *Poverty and Learning* (Eugene, Ore.: ERIC Clearinghouse on Educational Management, May 1993). ERIC No. ED357433.
5. Office of Educational Technology, op. cit.

6. Ron Renchler, *Poverty and Learning* (Eugene, Ore.: ERIC Clearing-house on Educational Management, May 1993). ERIC No. ED357433.

7. National Gambling Impact Study Commission, *Lotteries* (Washington, D.C., 1999). http://www.ngisc.gov/

Chapter 8

Student Health and Education

Poor health affects student learning. This obvious truth is confirmed not only by many studies, but by common sense and experience. When students are in poor health, negative effects may include cognitive and socioemotional deficits; low scores on developmental, achievement, and teacher-developed tests; and inattentiveness in class. Everyone has been unwell at some time and has experienced to a certain degree the effects that illness has on learning. Commonly the illness is a simple cold or flu that causes the student to be less able in the classroom or to miss a few days of school. In most cases the missed work is later completed and there are few, if any, long-term consequences.

Of major concern for educators are health problems with associated risks and damaging outcomes that are long-lasting. Long-term health concerns that affect cognitive and emotional development have a variety of causes and may occur at any age. Some occur even before birth, caused by lack of prenatal care or substance abuse by the mother. Other problems begin in the first few years of life, caused by such factors as low birth weight, malnutrition, sensory impairments, high blood lead levels, not receiving required vaccinations at the appropriate time, and anemia. When children who experience these problems arrive at school at age five or six, their poor health makes learning virtually impossible. The number of children beginning school in less than optimal health and unready to learn caused Congress to address the issue of health in the Goals 2000: Educate America Act of 1993.[1]

National Goals and Health Issues

The first of the six national education goals listed in the Educate America Act states, "By the year 2000, all children in America will start school ready to learn." Clearly such a goal is idealistic, rather than realistic. The year 2000 has come and gone, and not all children can start school ready to learn. To accomplish this goal at any time in the future, all children must receive appropriate nutrition and health care to begin school with healthy minds and bodies.

The federal government has several programs, managed by the U.S. Department of Health and Human Services, that address the health and nutritional needs of preschool-age children. Examples of these programs include the Maternal and Child Health Block Grant Program, Medicaid, and Project Head Start. Funds designated for the Maternal and Child Health Block Grant Program provide poor women and children with prenatal care, immunizations, nutritional services, and health screening. Medicaid also pays for the health care of low-income children and families by funding immunizations, vision and hearing tests, and dental care. And to improve the social and education abilities of low-income children, Project Head Start provides families with education, social, and health services. In addition, the Supplemental Food Program for Women, Infants, and Children, administered by the Department of Agriculture, provides supplemental foods and nutritional information to families with nutritionally at-risk children up to five years of age. Many of these federal programs are managed by the states and are jointly funded. During the 1990s, several states also developed their own programs to serve the health, nutrition, and education needs of preschool-age children.[2]

Even with the many state and federal government programs, many young children do not receive adequate health care. This is demonstrated by the increased number of reported cases of preventable diseases, such as measles and mumps. If children were properly immunized, occurrences of measles and mumps would be decreasing, not increasing. To reverse this trend, several organizations developed plans to improve the immunization status of preschool-age children. One such organization, the National Health/Education Consortium, established a multimedia program to educate parents and other caregivers about the correlation between health and learning. Their campaign included videos that highlighted the importance of prenatal care, nutrition, frequent health screening, and immunizations. Also included in the campaign were note pads with facts and messages for parents and public service announcements in the media. Additional programs included health clinics located in low-income neighborhoods that provide free or low-cost health care to patients. These clinics often provide acute medical and dental care, medical examinations, health education, and transportation.[3]

These programs helped numerous low-income children during the 1990s, but many qualified children were not helped and did not receive health-related services. For a variety of reasons, the parents of these children refrained from using the programs. Reasons given by parents included lack of transportation, conflicts with work, the child was not ill, and they did not have the time. Unfortunately, in some instances the parents were not concerned about the child's well-being.

A majority of low-income children are in some type of out-of-home childcare program, and so many states and organizations are now attempting to provide health care needs at these facilities. This strategy can be viewed as a way of answering parents' inability or reluctance to accept other programs. The American Public Health Association and the American Academy of Pediatrics jointly developed and published a useful set of standards that address health issues at daycare centers. Topics of interest include: staff health, health education, health protection and promotion, infectious diseases, ill children, and nutrition.[4]

Programs designed to promote and support the health of children must continue throughout the school-age years. This includes services ranging from providing low-income students with free or reduced-cost meals to arranging comprehensive health care for students on the school campus or through an association with a local clinic.

Promoting and Teaching Good Health

In the majority of states, the education codes mandate some type of health education. But the extent of such health instruction varies greatly. Some students receive planned, sequential, extensive health care instruction all through their school career, and other students receive health care education in only one grade. For other students, their only health instruction is the health "hot topic" of the moment, such as drug abuse or sexually transmitted disease. What all students require is a health program that prepares them to become responsible for their health decisions and practices. This includes instruction on how to provide healthy control of the environment, how to prevent and control communicable diseases, and how to identify and correct health problems that interfere with learning.[5]

A 1992 joint study by the Association for the Advancement of Health Education and the American School Health Association stated, "Lack of teacher training has been identified through national surveys as one of the most significant barriers to the effective implementation of school health education, especially at the elementary level."[6] Although a majority of states require teachers to be certified to teach health education at the secondary level, only one state in 1990 required certification at the elementary school level. To help prepare teachers in health education, the National Commission for Health Education Credentialing developed a certification program independent of state requirements. A teacher with a bachelor's degree in health education may take the certification exam and, if successful, he or she will receive a credential as a certified health education specialist. Although the credential is separate from state certification, it does indicate that the teacher has been competently prepared to teach a health education course.[7]

Studies indicate that young people make superior health judgments as a result of receiving health instruction. Schools are the logical place to provide health information and a healthful environment. When students have health care instruction, they are less likely to drink, smoke, take drugs, ride with drunk drivers, or become pregnant than are students who do not receive adequate health instruction. These negative behaviors are prevalent in the secondary school population. For example, according to the 1987 National Adolescent Student Health Survey of 10th-graders, 89% stated that they used alcohol, 35% had used marijuana, 8% had used cocaine, 40% ate breakfast fewer than three days a week, and only 45% knew that birth-control pills do not prevent the spread of sexually transmitted diseases.[8] Thus it seems a simple truth that every school should incorporate into the curriculum a comprehensive health education program taught by qualified professionals. That program should include health knowledge, health-related skills, wellness education, and other matters that reflect local concerns. Specific topics should involve community health, consumer health, family life, environmental health, personal health, emotional health, disease prevention, chronic illness, and substance abuse. Of course, each of these topics should be presented according to the age and maturity of the students.

Health Issues Debates

The topic of health education has caused spirited debates. Some areas of contention have included the teaching and content of sex education courses, school-based distribution of condoms, and student privacy versus parental knowledge. For example, people with a conservative worldview state that the central theme of sex education courses should be abstinence from sexual relations until marriage and that the distribution of condoms at school conveys to students that sex outside of marriage is a legitimate activity. Others, with a more liberal worldview, assert that because students are sexually active, teaching students to use condoms and to take other precautionary measures helps prevent unwanted pregnancies and the spread of sexually transmitted diseases. The rebuttal, of course, is that condoms are not 100% effective and the only way to ensure there will not be a pregnancy or sexual disease transmission is to refrain from having sex. Both views are correct in some sense, but which view will prevail in terms of curriculum and instruction is the real question.

Curricula have been developed that support both views. Because subject matter decisions are made locally, some schools in an area might teach abstinence-based sex education courses while nearby schools will teach how to practice "safe sex," or "safer sex," as the phrase is often rendered. Even the assessment of each curriculum is sometimes based on politics, instead of education concerns. For example, when the pregnancy rate of unmarried teenage females declined in the late 1990s, the supporters of both the abstinence and the safe-sex curricula claimed credit for the decline. Conservatives contended that teaching abstinence had influenced an increasing number of teenagers to delay becoming sexually active. Their liberal counterparts maintained that sexual activity had not declined but that the decrease in pregnancy was caused by students practicing safe sex. It should be noted that during this time, there was a movement in the schools in which many students publicly stated that virginity was a valid lifestyle and they were waiting until marriage before becoming sexually active. This does not indicate that overall sexual activity decreased, but that students who were not sexually active were empowered to voice their beliefs in the public square.

Another major area of contention concerns whether parents should be informed about what is being taught in health classes and what medical options are being advocated. For example, some parents have complained about the teaching of what they allege is "homosexual lifestyle advocacy" in health classes. These parents often have a worldview that considers homosexuality a sin and claim that teaching about homosexuality is not a health issue, but a lifestyle and political issue. One counter-argument is that regardless of the acceptability of a "homosexual lifestyle," there are students who are gay or lesbian — or whose parents, other family members, friends, or classmates are gay — and who need to understand health issues associated with sexual orientation. Some parents believe equally strongly that homosexuals must be accepted for who they are and must not be made the victims of societal ignorance, generalized homophobia, and violence. Parents on all sides often agree on one thing: They want access to what is being taught, and they want to be allowed to remove their child from class sessions if the content conflicts with their family's moral standards.

Perhaps an even greater concern for many parents arises when their child receives medical advice at school and the parents are not informed. An example is when a female student has an unplanned pregnancy and is advised to have an abortion, and the parents are not notified. Supporters of not informing the parents state that this is a privacy issue, and it is the student's choice whether the parent should be told. If school counselors were required to inform parents regarding issues stated to them in confidence, there would be a loss of trust and students would not seek their counsel and advice. Those who disagree on this point argue that certain issues extend beyond the scope of school counseling and must be discussed within the home. Terminating a pregnancy is one of those issues, they aver, and parents should certainly be involved in making such a decision. However, when confronted with the possibility that the parent may harshly discipline or even harm the student when so notified, the debate takes on a new dimension.

All of the debates I have mentioned here are rooted in the 20th century and show no signs of easy resolution as the 21st century begins.

Disabilities, Chronic Illnesses, and the School

Another health sphere in which educators often are directly involved is when a student has a disability or a chronic illness. As a result of the Individuals with Disabilities Education Act, passed by the U.S. Congress in 1997, schools are educating a greater number than ever before of students who have complex health needs that require case management and clinical services. Historically, a school nurse provided health services to students; but this role has changed in recent years, in part because of an increasing student-nurse ratio. Although the American Nursing Association advises a student-nurse ratio of one nurse for 750 students, many schools and districts provide only one nurse for more than 1,000 students.[9]

Consequently, the teacher has become a vital member of the disabled or chronically ill student's health care team. Because children and adolescents spend an average of 35 hours each week in school, teachers and other educators work with young people more often and for a longer time than anyone else outside the home. In fact, an elementary classroom teacher may spend more time actively communicating with many children than their parents can spend during the few awake hours at home before and after school. Therefore teachers often are the first to notice physical, behavioral, or emotional changes in their students. Such changes may indicate that some form of health-related intervention is needed. Although teachers are not medical professionals, they should have the basic training, knowledge, and skills necessary to recognize the health care needs of their students and to intervene when necessary. This includes knowing what to do in a medical emergency and how to refer the students to any required special services.[10]

Most teachers will face the challenges of teaching one or more students who have a physical disability or a chronic illness. According to the 1992 National Health Interview Survey, approximately 9% of the students reported that they had some type of physical disability. Disabilities ranged from being hearing or sight impaired to being confined to a wheelchair or bedridden. In addition, information from the Department of Health and Human Services indicates that approximately 1%, or more than one million, of the children in the United States have a severe chronic illness. These are students whose lives are limited by severe asthma, arthritis, cancer, diabetes, cystic fibrosis, epilepsy, HIV/AIDS, sickle cell disease, or other conditions. When chronic illness is defined as a condition that is expected to last more than three months and limits school performance, about 5% of all students qualify as chronically ill.[11]

Having a chronic illness or physical disability greatly influences the affected student's relationships, emotions, self-esteem, feelings of security, and independence. Acute, short-term illnesses, such as the common cold or flu, may produce similar effects; but the physical, lifestyle, and emotional changes that take place are usually temporary. Changes caused by a chronic illness or a disability typically are permanent. Indeed, society's attitudes toward chronic illnesses and disabilities convey a sense of permanence. A person with diabetes is called a *diabetic*, for example — the person becomes the disease or disability.

Teachers can help limit the negative social and emotional effects of a disability or a chronic illness by recognizing that the student is *not* the disease. After all, the student who has the flu is not classified as a "fluic." The student is simply a person who has the flu. In a similar spirit, a student with diabetes should not be labeled "the diabetic" but should be seen as merely a student who happens to have diabetes. This simple distinction will help the student to not base their identity on illness or disability, and this attitude also will be conveyed to other students. Chronic illnesses and disabilities cannot and should not be ignored. However, while they are part of the affected student's life, they are not the most important part.

Practical Applications of Law

Although schools and districts may vary in the level of available health care assistance, federal law requires every public school to provide adequate services for students with disabilities. Under federal law, chronic illnesses usually are considered a disability; and people with such illnesses are legally protected from discrimination. Federal laws require public schools to provide students with disabilities a free, appropriate education in the least restrictive environment. Special services, based on the disability and its effects, also are ensured. These services may include transportation, audiology, recreation, school health services, psychological services, physical and occupational therapy, speech and language therapy, assistive technology, and social work services.

When a school's administration is advised that a student has a disability or chronic illness, personnel must evaluate the student's special needs and develop a plan that will satisfy any medical requirements. This plan, known as an "individual education plan," is developed by school personnel working with sociologists, psychologists, medical specialists, and parents. Each student's needs are assessed, and the individual education plan defines how the school will deliver the services and assistance the student requires in order to have equitable access to all school programs. The plan must be updated, approved, and signed by the parent or guardian each academic year. Once in place, the individual education plan cannot be altered without parent consent. In addition, a member of the school faculty or staff is assigned to implement the plan and to inform other school personnel of their responsibilities under the plan.

Like their peers, students with a disability or chronic illness require love, support, understanding, and the full benefits of education. Classroom or school modifications may be required because of physical limitations, but these accommodations should not receive undo attention. An example of such a modification might be simply arranging for a friend of a student with arthritis to carry the affected student's books or providing a second set of textbooks for the student's home so that books would not have to be carried between home and school. Another example is adjusting assignment deadlines for students with cancer to accommodate their treatment schedule.

Teachers should guard against becoming overprotective. Students with a disability or chronic illness should be evaluated in terms of academics and discipline using the same standards applied to the rest of the class. Doing so helps instill in the affected student a pride in learning and also helps establish a camaraderie among all students. Adolescent students, in particular, want to feel as though they are part of the class and not different or abnormal. Even when a student's medical condition precludes full-time attendance, teachers should include that student in as many activities as possible. Depending on the situation, assignments can be sent home or to the hospital, the school can provide a tutor, or the student can attend school part of the day.

All students experience physical, psychological, and social pressures; but having a physical disability or a chronic illness can cause additional anxiety and apprehension. Such factors as recurrent pain, hospitalization, therapeutic procedures, school absences, and illness-related financial pressures may produce feelings of worry, inferiority, hopelessness, or guilt. Some students adapt well to the stresses, but others do not. Teachers should be alert to learning and behavioral changes that may result from such stresses and report them to the professionals involved in the student's health care. By communicating with parents and health care professionals, teachers will be better able to develop interventions that can minimize the student's frustrations with school and increase confidence and self-esteem.

The Problem of Violence

Another element that influences student health and learning is violence. Although school violence has been addressed previously, student safety cannot be disassociated from student health. School violence always has a detrimental effect on health and learning. For example, 13% of students responding to the 1987 National Adolescent Student Health Survey reported that they had been physically attacked during the past year at school or on a school bus. Six percent of the females stated that during the previous year someone had tried to force them to have sex while at school. Twenty-three percent of the boys said they carried a knife at least once during the past year to protect themselves, and 7% reported carrying a knife daily. Three percent of the boys declared that they carried a handgun to school at least one time during the past year, and 1% said that carrying a gun to school was a daily occurrence.[12]

As the 1980s progressed into the 1990s, a paradox occurred in American society. Although crime in society as a whole decreased each year during the century's final decade, reports of violence in schools, especially the well-publicized shootings of the late 1990s, indicated that school violence was increasing. Between 1 October 1997 and 21 May 1999, there were nine major assaults in U.S. schools that shocked the nation. These acts of injury did not transpire at schools where conventional wisdom might anticipate violence would occur. The news did not emanate from central Los Angeles, Chicago's south side, or New York City. The tragedies happened at locations that most people, including those at the schools, considered safe. In the first incident, on 1 October 1997 a 16-year-old boy in Pearl, Mississippi, killed his mother and two students and injured seven others. Other shootings occurred in Paducah, Kentucky, where three students were killed; Jonesboro, Arkansas, where four girls and a teacher were shot to death; Edinboro, Pennsylvania, where a teacher was killed; Fayetteville, Tennessee, where one student died; Springfield, Oregon, where two died at the school in addition to the alleged killer's parents; Notus, Idaho, where almost miraculously no one was injured; Littleton, Colorado, where the melee left 14 students and one teacher dead; and Conyers, Georgia, where six were injured. During this period, as if to make matters worse, educators at various schools throughout the country also received phone calls warning that acts of violence were planned for their schools.[13]

People representing different philosophical views declared in the public square various and often predictable reasons for the violence and how they believed the violence could be stopped. For example, those supporting gun control stated that the shootings occurred because guns are too accessible in society. People with conservative religious beliefs stated that the increased violence was attributable to a culture moving away from its presumed Judeo-Christian roots toward secularism and the removal of God from the public schools. Some faulted violence in the movies, on television, and in videogames or on lack of parental supervision. Others warned that "pointing fingers" and assigning blame were unproductive and that people should spend their energy finding solutions. Still other groups contended that some of the alleged causes for the violence in schools were not the problem and that society must carefully evaluate what is required so that fundamental individual rights are not lost. One illustration was the argument of the National Rifle Association that guns are not the cause of recent school violence because arms have always been available in society, there are adequate laws to prohibit the wrong people from obtaining guns, and the right to bear arms is a fundamental right in the United States.

Although assessing the reasons for problems in society and education is often a difficult and painful task, it has to be performed if solutions are to be discovered. It is improbable that solutions will be discovered if the purported roots of a problem are not honestly addressed. If criticism is valid, so be it. Accept responsibility, make changes, and continue. Addressing these important issues requires all in society to work together at the local, state, and national levels; to explore candidly the various explanations; and to discover solutions.

Safe Schools, Healthy Students

To address the health and safety issues caused by violence in the schools, on 1 April 1999 the U.S. Department of Education initiated the Safe Schools, Healthy Students Initiative. The purpose of the program was to "target youth with comprehensive services to prevent violence and promote healthy development." Under the initiative, more than $300 million will be awarded to 50 communities to link existing and newly developed services and activities to provide a comprehensive approach to violence prevention and healthy child development. Community proposals under this program require a formal partnership at the local level between the school district, law enforcement, local mental health units, family members, juvenile justice officials, and other relevant community-based organizations. To be considered comprehensive, the plan must address a safe school environment, alcohol and other drug prevention, school and community mental health intervention, early childhood development programs, education reform, and safe school policies.[14]

The Safe Schools, Healthy Students Initiative emanated from the White House Conference on School Safety held in October 1998. Attendees noted that studies indicate that a "comprehensive integrated community-wide approach is an effective way to promote healthy childhood development and address the problems of school violence and drug abuse."[15] No group working in isolation, whether law enforcement, the school, health professionals, or parents, will be able to solve the problem. It takes a community and public effort. Although studies from the 1990s indicate that too many children were not receiving the opportunity for a healthy start in life, this program aims to change that fact. According to the Surgeon General of the United States, the goal of this initiative is to provide children with a better chance in life by giving them an environment that is healthy, educationally stimulating, free of violence and abuse, free of stress, and free from harmful substances.

Notes

1. Bernard Cesarone, *Health Care, Nutrition, and Goal One* (Urbana: Children's Research Center, University of Illinois at Urbana-Champaign, 1993).

2. Kirk Winters, *Safe Schools, Healthy Students Initiative* (Washington, D.C.: U.S. Department of Education, 1999). http://www.ed.gov/MailingLists/EdInfo/Archive/msg00448.html

3. National Health/Education Consortium (NHEC), *Bridging the Gap: A Health Care Primer for Educational Professionals* (Washington, D.C.: National Commission to Prevent Infant Mortality and Institute for Effective Leadership, 1992).

4. American Public Health Association and American Academy of Pediatrics, *Caring for Our Children: National Health and Safety*

Performance Standards: Guidelines for Out-of-Home Child Care Programs (Washington, D.C., and Elk Grove Village, Ill., 1992). ERIC No. ED 344 674.

5. Liane Summerfield, "Comprehensive School Health Education," *ERIC Digest* (November 92): 1-4. ERIC No. ED 351335.

6. "Health Instruction Responsibilities and Competencies for Elementary (K-6) Classroom Teachers," *Journal of Health Education* 23 (September-October 1992): 352-54.

7. American Public Health Association and American Academy of Pediatrics, op. cit.

8. Centers for Disease Control, "Results from the National Adolescent School Health Survey," *MMWR Weekly* 38 (1989): 147-50.

9. Michael Stewart, "School Nurses: Who Is Caring for Our Nation's Children?" *American Nurse* 30 (May-June 1998): 8-11.

10. Dorothy Wishnietsky and Dan Wishnietsky, *Managing Chronic Illness in the Classroom* (Bloomington, Ind.: Phi Delta Kappa Educational Foundation, 1996).

11. National Institutes of Health, U.S. Department of Health and Human Services, *National Health Interview Survey, 1992* (Pittsburgh, Pa.: U.S. Government Printing Office, 1992).

12. Centers for Disease Control, op. cit.

13. Associated Press, "Assaults on U.S. Schools," 21 April 1999.

14. Kirk Winters, op. cit.

15. Office of the Press Secretary, the White House, "Promoting a Community-Wide Response to School Safety and Youth Violence," in *1998 White House Education Press Releases and Statements* (Washington, D.C., 1998), p. 1.

Chapter 9

Lifelong Learning

During the 1990s the phrases "lifelong learning" and "lifelong education" became common slogans among educators, politicians, and the general public. The common view was that because changes in society were occurring at a rapid pace, education must continue beyond traditional schooling for people to be successful citizens. For most of the history of the United States, this was not the case. Change happened at a slower pace, and often having only an elementary or secondary school education was enough to survive and even prosper in American culture. Most people lived their entire life in the same community and worked for 30 or more years for the same company or on the same farm. This pattern of life altered during the second half of the 20th century as advances in technology led to rapid and dramatic changes in society. Instead of living in the same area for a lifetime, people changed jobs and residences every few years. Population transience increased. This became a particularly common occurrence during the 1980s and 1990s as companies downsized to decrease costs or workers accepted higher-paying positions outside their current place of employment.

The most often used context for discussing lifelong learning is employment. For example, the Vice President of the United States stated in a 1997 speech that, according to the Commission for a Nation of Lifelong Learners, about 75% of current workers would require significant retraining over the next decade. To meet the requirements of these workers, the federal government initiated several programs to help ensure that all Americans would be able to keep learning and earning over their working years. One endeavor was led by the National Economic Council to determine how federal programs and initiatives could better support lifelong learning through the use of technology. In addition, the Department of Labor initiated the "American Career Kit," a series of four Internet-based tools to help workers find skilled jobs, along with required education and training. The career kit incorporated websites that provided information on education and training opportunities nationwide, information on wages, job growth projections by area and region, job-related resources ranging from job search tips to relocation guides, a résumé service, and a database listing current job vacancies.[1]

The Lifelong Learning Concept

Lifelong learning is not just about jobs and employment. It has many dimensions and involves the process of transforming experience into knowledge, skills, and attitudes about every aspect of life. These may include the sociological, psychological, religious, political, and other perspectives that involve the growth and development of individuals. Also, as the term *lifelong learning* implies, life experience and awareness does not take place only during adulthood, but begins at birth and ends at death. From the moment of birth, people are influenced by their environment and their experiences. Learning is a dynamic and continuing process throughout life.

For a majority of people, a major portion of lifelong learning consists of receiving a formal education by enrolling in courses at various categories of schools. These include elementary and secondary schools for the vast majority, followed for many by some form of adult education in community colleges, vocational or technical institutes, colleges and universities, specialty schools, or other formalized instruction ventures. Although some people engage in formal education simply for their own enrichment, the goal most often is a diploma, degree, or certificate. In most instances, the instructors are professional educators with expertise and credentials in their subject area. The schools are bureaucratic and formal, and it is the educators who control the content and format for learning.

But lifelong education is not limited to formal institutions. A variety of other organizations provide individuals with learning opportunities, though education may not be their primary purpose. For example, daycare centers provide experiential learning for infants and toddlers during the preschool years. The local library might sponsor a workshop on stock market investing for anyone with interest and a bit of discretionary income. Senior citizen centers sometimes offer aerobics classes designed for people 60 years of age or classes on nutrition for seniors. Similar programs can be found at YMCAs or YWCAs, religious institutions, service clubs, museums, correctional institutions, and a variety of other organizations. In most cases, children and adults participate for life enrichment, not to earn a credential or a degree. Adult participation usually is completely voluntary, and classes usually are less formal than at schools and colleges. However, many schools now are providing nonformal education opportunities in addition to their degree programs.

Because attendance in nonformal educational programs is voluntary and for enrichment, students often influence what classes are offered, in what setting, and when the classes take place. The instructors may be professionally trained or simply knowledgeable because of life experiences. Although the quality of nonformal education varies, learners rank such opportunities overall as beneficial in helping them reach their goals.[2]

Although not often thought of as part of lifelong learning, the majority of adult education takes place informally during the normal course of living. People of all ages continue learning by reading books and newspapers, through conversations with friends and family, by listening to the radio or tapes, by watching videos and television, and through various forms of self-directed learning. Individuals interact with others and learn from whatever materials and information come to hand. This experiential learning may be unintentional, or it may be planned, guided by an individual's interests and learning style. Thus such learning is both self-aware and instinctual.

Self-awareness of lifelong learning can — and proponents would say, must — be instilled in students at an early age. Teachers can and should teach the skill of learning how to learn. Transformations in society and the growing body of contextual knowledge require that all persons become agents of their individual education and learn how to adapt and change when necessary. Not infrequently, change is motivated internally by the desire to be more effective or self-sufficient. At other times, people must adapt and change out of absolute necessity. External motivation, such as the need to learn in order to retain one's job, is the key factor. Thus it is essential for each individual to learn how to acquire essential skills and knowledge in order to meet internal or external goals. This requires people to recognize their learning needs and to formulate learning objectives and ways to achieve them, whether it means learning a new sport, taking up a new hobby, or beginning a new career at mid-life.[3]

Federal Goals

In September 1997, when the United States Department of Education published its strategic plan for 1998-2002, the objective of Goal 3 was to ensure that all Americans have access to postsecondary education and lifelong learning. It was noted in the strategic plan that, while higher education in the United States is highly respected throughout the world, almost 40% of American high school graduates do not enter college directly from high school. Also, postsecondary school enrollment and completion rate for blacks, Hispanics, and students from low- and middle-income families, though increasing, is significantly lower than for whites from high-income families. The report emphasized three areas in which progress had to be made to ensure all students access to education beyond high school: 1) Ensure that all students graduate from high school with the academic background, skills, and motivation to pursue postsecondary education; 2) make available essential financial resources and support services; and 3) provide a delivery system for these resources and services that is efficient, financially sound, and responsive to students' needs. Goal 3 continues with a discussion about the importance of lifelong learning with respect to the labor market. Examples of lifelong learning, according to the Department of Education, are graduate school, adult basic education, advanced technical training, and training in job-entry skills.[4]

For some, lifelong learning is of special importance. These include people with disabilities, workers who require job-retraining because of labor market changes, and adults who lack fundamental and necessary skills. For example, people with disabilities are twice as likely to be unemployed as people without a disability, and adults who have not graduated from high school are often working in low-paying jobs or are unemployed and receiving government support. The extent of the problem of adults lacking basic skills was illustrated in the National Adult Literacy Survey of 1992. According to that survey, more than 21% of adults 16 years of age and older lacked the basic reading and mathematics skills needed for higher-paying jobs or entry into higher education.[5]

As the United States enters the 21st century, the Department of Education is attempting to improve the quality of its rehabilitation and adult education programs. This includes, according to Goal 3, identifying best practices from the research and updating the performance data systems to provide feedback for program improvement. In addition, the Department of Education will work with other federal agencies to improve career placement for adults with disabilities or those who need basic skill education. One core strategy is a national campaign to motivate middle school students and parents to prepare for higher education. This campaign includes providing information about the benefits, academic requirements, and cost of higher education and the availability of financial aid and support services. The Department of

Education also will provide incentives and direction to help increase the coordination between secondary and postsecondary schools, strengthen existing programs, and implement ways to assist disadvantaged students. In addition, the department will use computer and information technologies to develop and implement a simple procedure to apply for financial aid and for receiving specific answers to financial aid questions.

Another core strategy addresses the importance of adults strengthening their skills and improving their earning power through lifelong learning. An educated workforce is beneficial to business and labor. Because the workplace is continually changing, most people have to upgrade their skills periodically and, at times, be retrained for a new job. The worker gains by having more productive years in a higher-paying job, and business profits by having access to a more flexible and better-trained workforce. To help provide financial support for adults returning to school, the Department of Education is endeavoring to make more adults aware of federal student aid programs, such as the Higher Education Act (Title IV) student aid program and the Lifetime Learning tax credit. Examples of tax credits, at the time of this writing, include allowing workers to exclude up to $5,250 of employer-provided education benefits from their income, establishing an education IRA, and receiving a 20% tax credit for the first $10,000 of college tuition and required fees paid each year by qualifying families beginning in 2003.

Education and Life

Although the Department of Education and other government lifelong learning programs of the late 20th and early 21st century have emphasized employment and economics, people's lives embody more than work and money. Education is linked to life itself, providing individuals with social, political, and psychological empowerment, enrichment, and an overall sense of self-fulfillment. Therefore, learning must extend beyond the role of work to influence a person's entire life — throughout the lifespan.

Learners should acquire the ability to identify and adapt to the changing intellectual demands of society and to life demands on themselves. What is learned should stimulate positive personal and emotional growth and a sense of true autonomy. In the divergent circumstances of life, the type of learning required often is discovered in the nonformal settings I previously described.

However, education institutions are becoming more involved in providing learning opportunities that are less formal and that look beyond the world of work. In an increasing number of postsecondary schools, more and more courses are being offered that are designed to provide "life enrichment." These courses may be part of the school's degree program or included in extension or continuing education programs. For example, community colleges, in addition to providing vocational, associate degree, and college transfer courses, often offer continuing education classes in such diverse subjects as ballroom dancing, how to buy a house, gardening, porcelain dollmaking, cake decorating, and so forth.

Also offered in the continuing education division of postsecondary schools are business-related classes that enable people to upgrade their work skills without entering a degree or certificate program. These classes are not limited to people active in the workplace. Students who merely desire to learn a new skill often fill these classes. Many of these classes involve the use of computer technology. For example, a class teaching web-based design offered in a university continuing education department might be aimed at the corporate professional, but among the students could well be a retiree who has enrolled to learn how to create and publish a web page about making teddy bears as a hobby.[6]

A significant challenge for colleges and universities when providing continuing education and corporate courses is to have the courses accessible to all potential students, not just the primary target group. Accessibility considerations include time and place. For example, many continuing education classes are scheduled for one evening a week or on Saturday, so that the class will not conflict with students' other responsibilities (primarily work, but also certain family obligations). Place also is an important variable because availability of transportation and commuting time can determine whether an interested student is able to enroll. Although most of the continuing education and corporate courses are taught at a school's main campus, a growing number of classes are being scheduled at off-campus sites, such as workplaces and community centers and libraries.

Computerized Continuing Education

With the advent of the 21st century and computer-based technologies, the Internet has become a delivery system for continuing, corporate, and degree courses. Instructors are creating multimedia lessons and publishing them on an Internet-based file server. Using a computer connected to the Internet, students are then able to access the course from any location. Formal and nonformal education ceases to be restricted to a particular place or time. Students use technology to gain access to video lectures and accompanying multimedia and interactive demonstrations and activities. Education, instead of being geographically fixed, is "located" wherever it is required by the omnipresence of so-called cyberspace. For example, employees who are seeking advanced training or undergraduate students who lack the time to attend on-campus courses can access an instructor's lecture asynchronously — in other words, not at the time it is actually being delivered — from any computer-equipped location: home, office, or "cyber cafe." Rigid schedules are a thing of the past with such technological access, and students can structure their own learning experience, for example, replaying parts of the lecture they did not understand or skipping topics with which they are already familiar. In addition to the lecture, the computer screen can display a virtual blackboard that has a graphic display of important points. Often associated with these classes is the ability to e-mail the instructor with questions or comments and to interact in online chat rooms with other students in the class.

Using technology, students located at a remote location also can attend lectures as they are being presented. These classes are broadcast live using the Internet, land-based microwave, or satellite technology. In many instances, the broadcast is two-directional. Students see the instructor and, using a camera at the student's site, the instructor is able to view the student and broadcast the student's image to other remote sites. The major benefit of live broadcasting is that students may ask questions and receive immediate feedback. This does not prevent e-mail questions at a later time or enjoying the benefits of a class-oriented chat room. Although the live lecture creates a class-time dependency, students often say that they welcome the instantaneous interaction with the instructor and the other students in the class.

With the advent of web-based courses, some educators have questioned the need for a local campus. This is similar to the statements some educators were making in the 1980s when they predicted that the computer would eliminate the need for teachers. Teachers were not replaced by computers, and having courses delivered by technology will not supplant the campus. For many students, especially those who are young adults, the college or university is more than its classes. It is a total life experience that helps bridge the distance between adolescence and adulthood. In addition to the academics, students on campus encounter financial, political, social, and other experiences that help them mature. These life-developing events are not fully available in virtual reality. It is vital that technology does not become so central to life that humans become "mushrooms," on the Internet for so many hours they never see the light of day.

There are other concerns regarding course distribution using technology. One major consideration is equity of access. With all the excitement of global access using the Internet, educators must not ignore the challenge of meeting the needs of all potential students. Internet access is still out of reach of some. This is yet another instance when a person's socioeconomic status has a direct effect on opportunities. Students from middle- to high-income backgrounds often have home computers connected to an Internet service provider and are easily able to access web-based classes. Low-income students are less likely to have a home environment that can financially support the purchase of a home computer or the monthly fee for Internet access. Supplemental access, say, at a public library may help bridge the gap between the haves and the have nots, but such access is limited and requires more effort to obtain. Several solutions have been proposed to make Internet access more readily available to low-income families, such as the federal government and a local telephone or cable company providing low-cost data lines and equipment that will enable access through the family television. But most such solutions to the problem are still in the thinking stage. Fortunately, as the cost of computers continues to decrease, an increasing number of low-income families are beginning to enjoy the benefits of this technology.

As the United States begins the 21st century, few would argue against the need for accessible and diverse education opportunities to address the many social, economic, and technical changes within society. Lifelong learning does not consist merely of personal health- and hobby-related classes taken by retired people, though the popularity of these types of courses continues to increase. Lifelong learning is for everyone, young and old and in between. It requires providing education at all levels and throughout people's lives, so that they can be optimally productive, whether at work or at leisure. Educators should teach students from early on to become agents of their own education and to be critical concerning what and why they learn. Colleges and universities, in particular, must be at the forefront of lifelong learning by opening their classes to the vast, diverse community of potential learners, rather than limiting their offerings to those who seek professional work and advancement. Above all, educators of every stripe should assist people from every economic status to learn throughout their lives.

Notes

1. The White House, Office of the Vice President, "Vice President Gore Announces New Administration Steps on Lifelong Learning,"

18 November 1997. http://www.ed.gov/PressReleases/11-1997/vppromot.html

2. Michael Galbraith, "Community-Based Organizations and the Delivery of Lifelong Learning Opportunities," paper presented to the National Institute on Postsecondary Education, Libraries, and Lifelong Learning, Office of Educational Research and Improvement, U.S. Department of Education, Washington, D.C., April 1995.

3. R. Smith, *Learning How to Learn* (New York: Cambridge University Press, 1982), p. 19.

4. U.S. Department of Education, *U.S. Department of Education Strategic Plan, 1998-2002: Goal 3. Ensure Access to Postsecondary Education and Lifelong Learning* (Washington, D.C., September 1997). http://www.ed.gov/pubs/StratPln/goal_3.html

5. Irwin S. Kirsch, Ann Jungeblut, Lynn Jenkins, and Andrew Kolstad, *Adult Literacy in America: A First Look at the Findings of the National Adult Literacy Survey* (Washington, D.C.: National Center for Education Statistics, 1993).

6. *Lifelong Learning, Technological Horizons in Education Journal* 26 (April 1999): entire issue.

Chapter 10

Toward the Future

Society has vested in educators the responsibility of providing individuals, children and adults alike, with the skills required for full citizenship, meaningful employment, and a productive life. To accomplish this task, they must transcend political ideologies that influence education, seeking instead the pragmatic and the practical. For example, a teacher must determine — given the particular circumstances of his or her teaching environment, subject, and students — the practical effects of a repertoire of teaching methods, deciding which methods among the many will most effectively increase students' skills, knowledge, and understanding. This is not accomplished by hewing to specific political, ideological, or philosophical beliefs, but by researching the outcomes of carefully controlled studies and by the conscious application of sound curricular and instructional principles.

Previously I mentioned the controversy in reading instruction that arose during the 1980s and 1990s over which was the better method: phonics or whole language instruction. Often that debate became politicized. But most thoughtful educators recognized (eventually) that their students would be better served by being treated as individuals with individual needs. Some students would be better served by greater emphasis on phonics, others by greater emphasis on whole language — most by some combination of the methods. Pedagogical motives, on the whole, are a sounder basis for education change than are political motives.

A Value for Debate

Some controversies that confront educators cannot be separated from the political climate of the time. One such current topic concerns the separation of church and state and what part religion and the church can have in public education. This is hardly a new controversy, but it shows little sign of abating anytime soon. In 1963 the Supreme Court ruled that the establishment clause of the First Amendment made it unconstitutional for states to promote such activities as reading the Bible or institutionalizing prayer in schools (or at school-sponsored events).[1] Although there previously had been conflict between various political groups that supported or opposed prayer in schools, this case amplified the tension. Court battles have been waged, often with contradictory results; and it appears that no definitive settlement will be reached in the near future.

But education can and must be an endeavor of cooperation and compromise. People from the diverse philosophies represented in the church-state debate can work together to find common ground. Realizing the negative effect the argument over the separation of church and state was having on schooling, individuals from education, religion, government, and civil rights groups met in 1999 to establish guidelines that detailed how churches can be involved with public schools without violating the constitutional separation of church and state. People from such diverse groups as the American Jewish Congress, the Christian Legal Society, and the First Amendment Center at Vanderbilt University joined together to publish guidelines regarding religious expression and involvement in the public schools. Goals expressed by participants included public school students doing homework or participating in sports at a temple or church instead of dealing drugs on the street corner. Even the American Civil Liberties Union, which many people wrongly view of as being anti-religion, praised the effort.[2]

This example illustrates the importance of permitting diverse views to be discussed and debated in the public square. Unfortunately, in the 1990s an increasing number of individuals and groups not only presented their views but also attempted to block the presentation of opposing ideas. There were boycotts of sponsors of certain television or radio shows and sponsorships withdrawn over ideological issues, canceled conventions in certain cities because of election results, boycotts of theme parks and other businesses, and similar actions advocated and carried out by groups intent on squelching the rights of others. Letters to the editor complained about others' right to publish contrary views. The rhetoric often was caustic and vicious. Lack of civility in public debate was decried in all quarters, but to little effect, or so it seemed.

Strongly held beliefs engender strong emotions. But strong emotions cannot excuse civil discord. Many of the debates that affect education will not be settled easily. Nonetheless, the schools must move forward. Educators have a long and honored tradition of openness. What better place than the schools for an open public square to present, debate, and find solutions? If this is the case, the "political correctness" movement that developed on many university campuses during the late 20th century was not an acclamation for education, but a stain. Whenever educators decide which topics and beliefs should be allowed, rather than openly considering all topics, not only is education weakened, but so is society. This is not to say that all ideas and thoughts are of equal value. It does say that diverse thoughts and ideas should be heard so that they can be evaluated.

Diversity as a Strength

Hearing diverse views is essential in education because solutions frequently are discovered in the diversity. An example is the pedagogical debate concerning whether particular content to be learned in school is more or less important than acquiring the tools to enable future learning. This controversy, like many in education, has acquired political overtones. And the entry of politics into a debate tends to de-emphasize what is best for the students in favor of the politically "correct" or politically expedient. People who support topic-specific content knowledge state that to learn a topic well, a student must learn the relevant vocabulary, conventions, and schema that form the knowledge base. Without this knowledge base, critical thinking about a topic is not possible, because there is no starting point or foundation. In addition, critical thinking also is subject-specific. Just because a person can think critically about one topic, say, mathematics, does not translate into thinking critically about another topic, such as world literature.

Contrarians who emphasize teaching critical thinking tools and learning to learn, instead of the transmission of content knowledge, state that students use only a small percentage of the content they learn in school. In addition, knowledge is changing so rapidly that what is applicable today will soon be irrelevant. Skills that today's students require for life are not how to memorize facts but how to access information, solve problems, and learn new knowledge.

As with most scholarly disagreements, neither side is completely right or completely wrong. What is educationally sound tends, as usual, to be a blend of the ideas from diverse positions. Most educators agree that schools should teach both content knowledge and the skills required for lifelong learning. Technology-based courses provide a relevant example because most students understand that the discipline's current "facts" soon will be outdated. One has merely to read books on technology that were published only a few years ago to see that the "facts" read like artifacts. In their time, those facts were relevant. Moreover, they enabled technological improvements. Change came about because people understood the current knowledge and were able to build on that knowledge to develop new knowledge and technology. Both content knowledge and critical thinking skills were needed.

Education critics contend that educators must take responsibility for inferior schooling. But that is too simplistic. At best, educators can take responsibility only for doing their best, often against great societal odds, to provide their students with the knowledge and skills required for success in their local community and the culture in general. In fact, most schools today *are* preparing their students to meet the challenges of their world. Anyone who compares the content of current textbooks at all levels with those of only a few years ago will see a clear change toward more forward-looking material. For example, many chemistry books published in the 1980s emphasized memorization of facts from the periodic table and balancing chemical equations. Today's texts are supporting active learning, rather than rote. Students are learning about DNA and how ecology is affected by cultural and political decisions. Education critics need to examine more than scores on standardized tests; they should investigate the curriculum. A person who graduated with a chemistry degree only two decades ago could well have problems understanding the content of many high school and perhaps even middle-school science projects, so much has education changed.

Learning, Work, and the American Future

Most graduates of the American education system have acquired the skills needed for satisfactory and often well-paying jobs. Although many debate the true relationship between the quality of education and national economic health, it is safe to state that the quality of education in the United States provides students with the opportunity for gainful employment. This has been demonstrated by the increased number of people in highly skilled, high-paying jobs and the increased productivity of employees. Even companies that complain that they have to provide additional education for their newly hired graduates must at least admit that most of their new personnel have sufficient intellectual capital to successfully complete company-sponsored training. Much of the criticism of American public schools is unwarranted and unjustified.

However, no one can ignore the real problems involving education and economics. For example, an issue that must be resolved by society is the significant disparity in education and wages among the different groups in society. Teacher salaries are a well-publicized example, especially as prognosticators point to a coming teacher shortage and growing reluctance among college graduates to enter what they perceive as a low-paying career. Most people in both business and education believe that unless changes are made, the differences will increase and negative consequences will result.

Today's educators must continue to advance and promote a distinct vision for the future. The excitement of the new century and the new millennium inspired the futurist potential in just about everyone. To meet the challenges of education and to satisfy the requirements of their students, educators cannot be content with goals and objectives developed in the year 2000 (or any other previous year), however little they actually achieved. Goals, objectives, and target outcomes should continually be reviewed and updated to meet current needs and consider present education concerns. In addition, the procedures and programs established to address these issues should be assessed regularly to determine their effect. Programs that are successful should be continued and expanded. Programs that are not achieving their stated goals and objectives should be revised or discontinued. Too often in schools, programs that are failing to meet the needs of students are continued for political, social, or personal reasons. Failure often is blamed on lack of funding. Yes, more money *can* improve education; but the money has to be spent on programs that are pedagogically sound and successful, not socially or politically motivated.

Society has given teachers the vital, but sometimes frustrating, responsibility of providing students with the skills required for full citizenship, meaningful employment, and a productive life. The frustrations most often arise from the great responsibility placed on teachers, responsibility whose burden is made heavier by challenging changes in culture and demographics. The students are more diverse, parents seem less supportive of schools, there is more bureaucratic paperwork, and education questions that previously were academic are now sometimes political. Too many teachers feel overwhelmed, as though they are not making a difference; and they are abandoning the profession at a time when replacements are becoming scarce.

As the 21st century gets under way, American educators (and educators everywhere) must remember that they are touching and changing lives for the better, however beleaguered they feel. There is a story that has become a cliché, but it nonetheless is worth repeating. An individual — I like to think, a teacher — was walking along a beach covered with hundreds of starfish. With each step, this person reached down, picked up a starfish, and tossed it back into the ocean. An observer watched for a while and then asked, "Why bother? There are so many starfish and you are only saving a few. What difference is it making?" The starfish thrower reached down, picked up yet another starfish, and tossed it into the ocean. "It made a difference to that one."

Educators, in similar fashion, are making a difference one student at a time. In rich classrooms and in poor classrooms, in crowded settings and where there is ample room, teachers and administrators are making a difference for the students and their parents with whom they work directly and, indirectly, for communities and for the nation.

Notes

1. *Abington School District* v. *Schemp*; *Murray* v. *Curlett*, 374 U.S. 203, 1963.
2. Charles C. Haynes, Oliver S. Thomas, John B. Leach, and Alyssa Kendall, *Finding Common Ground: A First Amendment Guide to Religion and Public Education* (Nashville, Tenn.: First Amendment Center, 1998). http://www.freedomforum.org/newsstand/brochures/ printschools_communities.asp

Resources

The following list contains book-length resources on the topics addressed in each chapter. All of the references were published in 1995 or later and are written by authors from diverse worldviews. The beliefs and conclusions of many of these authors differ from the views expressed in this book. They are included to illustrate the varieties of opinion that are shaping the education dialogue today and for the immediate future.

Chapter 1: The Scene

Berman, Paul; Nelson, Beryl; Perry, Rebecca; Silverman, Debra; Solomon, Debra; and Kamprath, Nancy. *The State of Charter Schools: National Study of Charter Schools, Third-Year Report.* Washington, D.C.: U.S. Government Printing Office, 1999.

Bracey, Gerald W. *Setting the Record Straight: Responses to Misconceptions About Public Education in the United States.* Alexandria, Va.: Association for Supervision and Curriculum Development, 1997.

Chavers, Dean, ed. *Exemplary Programs in Indian Education.* 2nd ed. Albuquerque: Native American Scholarship Fund, 1996.

Choy, Susan P. *Public and Private Schools: How Do They Differ?* Findings from "The Condition of Education, 1997," No. 12. Washington, D.C.: U.S. Government Printing Office, 1997.

Doerr, Edd, et al. *The Case Against School Vouchers.* Amherst, N.Y.: Prometheus, 1996.

Freeman, Kassie, ed. *African American Culture and Heritage in Higher Education Research and Practice.* Westport, Conn.: Greenwood, 1998.

Gilkey, Langdon Brown. *Creationism on Trial: Evolution and God at Little Rock.* Studies in Religion and Culture. Charlottesville: University Press of Virginia, 1998.

Goodlad, John I., and McMannon, Timothy J., eds. *The Public Purpose of Education and Schooling.* San Francisco: Jossey-Bass, 1997.

Koetzsch, Ronald E. *The Parents' Guide to Alternatives in Education.* Boston: Shambhala, 1997.

Lipkin, Arthur. *Understanding Homosexuality, Changing Schools: A Text for Teachers, Counselors, and Administrators.* Boulder, Colo.: Westview, 1999.

McMannon, Timothy J. *Morality, Efficiency, and Reform: An Interpretation of the History of American Education.* Work in Progress Series No. 5. Seattle: Institute for Educational Inquiry, 1995.

McNeely, Margaret E., ed. *Guidebook to Examine School Curricula: TIMSS as a Starting Point to Examine Curricula.* Washington, D.C.: Office of Educational Research and Improvement, 1997. ERIC No. ED410128.

Menendez, Albert J. *Home Schooling: The Facts.* Silver Spring, Md.: Americans for Religious Liberty, 1996.

Miller, Ron, ed. *Educational Freedom for a Democratic Society: A Critique of National Standards, Goals, and Curriculum.* Brandon, Vt.: Resource Center for Redesigning Education, 1995.

Mitchell, Antoinette, and Raphael, Jacqueline. *Goals 2000: Case Studies of Promising Districts.* Washington, D.C.: U.S. Department of Education, Planning and Evaluation Service, 1999.

Morgan, Harry. *Historical Perspectives on the Education of Black Children.* Westport, Conn.: Praeger, 1995.

Saks, Judith B. *The Basics of Charter Schools: A School Board Primer.* Alexandria, Va.: National School Boards Association, Council of Urban Boards of Education, 1997. ERIC No. ED412609.

Swisher, Karen Gayton, and Tippeconnic, John W., III, eds. *Next Steps: Research and Practice to Advance Indian Education.* Charleston, W.V.: ERIC/CRESS, 1999.

Walling, Donovan R., ed. *Open Lives, Safe Schools: Addressing Gay and Lesbian Issues in Education.* Bloomington, Ind.: Phi Delta Kappa Educational Foundation, 1996.

Williams, L. Patricia, comp. *The Regulation of Private Schools in America: A State-by-State Analysis.* Washington, D.C.: U.S. Government Printing Office, 1996.

Wright, David E., III; Hirlinger, Michael W.; and England, Robert E. *The Politics of Second Generation Discrimination in American Indian Education: Incidence, Explanation, and Mitigating Strategies.* Westport, Conn.: Bergin & Garvey, 1998.

Chapter 2: Thinking Global

Appel, Morgan, et al. *The Impact of Diversity on Students. A Preliminary Review of the Research Literature.* Washington, D.C.: Association of American Colleges and Universities, 1996.

Bowser, Benjamin P., et al., eds. *Toward the Multicultural University.* Westport, Conn.: Greenwood, 1995.

Bruner, Charles, and Chang, Hedy Nai-Lin. *Valuing Diversity, Practicing Inclusion: A Matter of Commitment.* Community Collaboration Guidebook No. 3. Des Moines: Child and Family Policy Center, 1998.

Children's Privacy Protection and Parental Empowerment Act of 1996. Hearing on H.R. 3508 before the Subcommittee on Crime of the Committee on the Judiciary. House of Representatives, One Hundred Fourth Congress, Second Session. (12 September 1996). Washington, D.C.: U.S. Government Printing Office, 1997.

Cole, Robert W., ed. *Educating Everybody's Children: Diverse Teaching Strategies for Diverse Learners, What Research and Practice Say About Improving Achievement.* Alexandria, Va.: Association for Supervision and Curriculum Development, 1995.

Farrell, Glen M., ed. *The Development of Virtual Education: A Global Perspective. A Study of Current Trends in the Virtual Delivery of Education.* Burnaby, B.C.: Open Learning Agency, 1999.

Gibson, Joyce Taylor. *Developing Strategies and Practices for Culturally Diverse Classrooms.* Bill Harp Professional Teachers Library Series. Norwood, Mass.: Christopher-Gordon, 1998.

Hammrich, Penny L. "World View: Defining the Cultural Context of the Teacher." Paper presented at the Annual Meeting of the National Association for Research in Science Teaching, Boston, 28-31 March 1999.

Hurtado, Sylvia; Milem, Jeffrey; Clayton-Pedersen, Alma; and Allen, Walter. *Enacting Diverse Learning Environments: Improving the Climate for Racial/Ethnic Diversity in Higher Education.* ASHE-ERIC Higher Education Report Vol. 26, No. 8. Washington, D.C.: ERIC Clearinghouse on Higher Education, 1999.

Korbel, Linda A. *New Expeditions: Charting the Future of Global Education in Community Colleges.* Washington, D.C.: American Council on Education, 1998.

Rockwell, Robert E.; Andre, Lynda C.; and Hawley, Mary K. *Parents and Teachers as Partners: Issues and Challenges*. Orlando, Fla.: Harcourt Brace College Publishers, 1996.

Spring, Joel. *The Intersection of Cultures: Multicultural Education in the United States*. New York: McGraw-Hill, 1995.

Chapter 3: The Global Curriculum

Benjamin, Judy, et al. *Above and Beyond: Secondary Activities for Peace Corps Volunteers*. Washington, D.C.: Peace Corps Information Collection and Exchange, 1995.

Byrnes, Ronald S.; Downing, Peter W.; and Vogler, Carol. *Teaching About Africa: A Continent of Complexities*. Denver: Center for Teaching International Relations, University of Denver, 1996.

Merryfield, Merry M., ed. *Making Connections Between Multicultural and Global Education: Teacher Educators and Teacher Education Programs*. Washington, D.C.: AACTE Publications, 1996.

Raby, Rosalind Latiner. "Looking to the Future: Report on California Community College International and Global Education Programs, A Report on Activities Funded by the Chancellor's Office for the California Community Colleges 1997-1999." California Colleges for International Education, 1998.

Taylor, Howard E., ed. *Getting Started in Global Education: A Primer for Principals and Teachers*. Alexandria, Va.: National Association of Elementary School Principals, 1997.

Chapter 4: Technology and the Global Curriculum

Bazeli, Marilyn J., and Heintz, James L. *Technology Across the Curriculum: Activities and Ideas*. Englewood, Colo.: Libraries Unlimited, 1997.

Brody, Philip J. *Technology Planning and Management Handbook: A Guide for School District Educational Technology Leaders*. Englewood Cliffs, N.J.: Educational Technology Publications, 1995.

Czerneda, Julie, ed. *By Design: Technology Exploration and Integration*. rev. ed. Teachers Helping Teachers Series. Toronto: Trifolium, 1996.

De Cicco, Eta; Farmer, Mike; and Hargrave, James. *Using the Internet in Secondary Schools*. Herndon, Va.: Stylus, 1998.

King, Tom, ed. *Technology in the Classroom: A Collection of Articles.* Arlington Heights, Ill.: IRI/SkyLight, 1997.

Latchem, Colin, and Lockwood, Fred, eds. *Staff Development in Open and Flexible Learning.* Routledge Studies in Distance Education Series. New York: Routledge, 1998.

National Educational Technology. *Standards for Students.* Eugene, Ore.: ISTE, 1998.

Sivin-Kachala, Jay; Bialo, Ellen R.; and Langford, Jonathan. *The Effectiveness of Technology in Schools, '90-'97 Report.* Washington, D.C.: Software Publishers Association, 1997.

Skeele, Linda, ed. *Teaching Information Literacy Using Electronic Resources for Grades K-6.* Worthington, Ohio: Linworth, 1996.

Treadwell, Mark. *1001 of the Best Internet Sites for Educators, K-College.* Arlington Heights, Ill.: SkyLight, 1999.

Webb, L. Dean. *Integrating Technology in the High School: Breaking Ranks, Making It Happen.* Reston, Va.: National Association of Secondary School Principals, 1999.

Chapter 5: Diversity and Equity

Benjamin, Michael. *Cultural Diversity, Educational Equity and the Transformation of Higher Education: Group Profiles as a Guide to Policy and Programming.* Westport, Conn.: Greenwood, 1996.

Daugherty, Dorothy, and Stanhope, Victoria, eds. *Pathways to Tolerance: Student Diversity.* Bethesda, Md.: National Association of School Psychologists, 1998.

Gibson, Joyce Taylor. *Developing Strategies and Practices for Culturally Diverse Classrooms.* Bill Harp Professional Teachers Library Series. Norwood, Mass.: Christopher-Gordon, 1998.

Jones-Wilson, Faustine C., et al., eds. *Encyclopedia of African-American Education.* Westport, Conn.: Greenwood, 1996.

Kendall, Frances E. *Diversity in the Classroom: New Approaches to the Education of Young Children.* 2nd ed. New York: Teachers College Press, 1996.

Martin, Renee J., ed. *Practicing What We Teach: Confronting Diversity in Teacher Education.* Albany: State University of New York Press, 1995.

Olmscheid, Carey. "Parental Involvement: An Essential Ingredient." 1999. ERIC No. ED431044.

Robbins, John, ed. *The ABC's of Parent Involvement in Education: Preparing Your Child for a Lifetime of Success.* 2nd ed. Washington, D.C.: National Parents' Day Coalition, 1998.

Rooney, Charles, and Schaeffer, Bob. *Test Scores Do Not Equal Merit: Enhancing Equity & Excellence in College Admissions by Deemphasizing SAT and ACT Results.* Cambridge, Mass.: FairTest, 1998.

White House Initiative on Educational Excellence for Hispanic Americans. *Our Nation on the Fault Line: Hispanic American Education.* Washington, D.C., 1996.

Chapter 6: Ideology, Politics, and Education

Blumberg, Jonathan A.; Dowling, Ruth T.; Horton, Janet L.; Howie, Margaret-Ann F.; Majestic, Ann L.; Schwartz, Richard A.; Shaw, Brian C.; and Smith, Bruce W. *Legal Guidelines for Curbing School Violence.* Alexandria, Va.: National School Boards Association, 1995.

Bonilla, Carlos A., and Goss, Joyce, eds. *Students at Risk: The Teachers' Call to Action!* Stockton Calif.: ICA, 1997.

Finch, Curtis R., and Crunkilton, John R. *Curriculum Development in Vocational and Technical Education: Planning, Content, and Implementation.* 5th ed. Needham Heights, Mass.: Allyn & Bacon, 1999.

Flannery, Daniel J. *School Violence: Risk, Preventive Intervention, and Policy.* Urban Diversity Series No. 109. New York: ERIC Clearinghouse on Urban Education, 1997.

Glyer, Diana, and Weeks, David L., eds. *The Liberal Arts in Higher Education: Challenging Assumptions, Exploring Possibilities.* Lanham, Md.: University Press of America, 1998.

Johnston, Lloyd D.; O'Malley, Patrick M.; and Bachman, Jerald G. *National Survey Results on Drug Use from the Monitoring the Future Study, 1975-1998. Volume I: Secondary School Students.* Washington, D.C.: U.S. Government Printing Office, 1999.

Kadel, Stephanie; Watkins, Jim; Follman, Joseph; Hammond, Cathy. *Reducing School Violence: Building a Framework for School Safety.* 3rd ed. Tallahassee, Fla.: SERVE, 1999.

Kimball, Bruce A., and Orrill, Robert, eds. *The Condition of American Liberal Education: Pragmatism and a Changing Tradition, An Essay with Commentaries and Responses.* New York: College Board, 1995.

Lynch, Richard L. *Designing Vocational and Technical Teacher Education for the 21st Century: Implications from the Reform Literature.*

Information Series No. 368. Columbus, Ohio: Center on Education and Training for Employment, 1997.

Making the Grade: A Guide to School Drug Prevention Programs, Preventing Alcohol, Tobacco and Other Drug Use. Washington, D.C.: Drug Strategies, 1999.

Merriam, Sharan B., ed. *Selected Writings on Philosophy and Adult Education.* 2nd ed. Melbourne, Fla.: Krieger, 1995.

Mertz, Gayle. *Diversity and the Law.* Lawyers in the Classroom Series. Chicago: American Bar Association, 1995.

Nash, Robert J. *Answering the "Virtuecrats": A Moral Conversation on Character Education.* Advances in Contemporary Educational Thought Volume 21. New York: Teachers College Press, 1997.

A Nation "Still" at Risk: An Education Manifesto. Washington, D.C.: Thomas B. Fordham Foundation, 1998. ERIC No. ED422455.

Pool, Harbison, and Page, Jane A., eds. *Beyond Tracking: Finding Success in Inclusive Schools.* Bloomington, Ind.: Phi Delta Kappa Educational Foundation, 1995.

Stein, Nan D. *Classrooms and Courtrooms: Facing Sexual Harassment in K-12 Schools.* New York: Teachers College Press, 1999.

Volokh, Alexander, and Snell, Lisa. *School Violence Prevention: Strategies to Keep Schools Safe.* Policy Study No. 234. Los Angeles: Reason Public Policy Institute, 1997.

Chapter 7: Economics and Education

Bauer, David G., et al. *Educator's Internet Funding Guide: Classroom Connect's Reference Guide to Technology Funding.* Lancaster, Pa.: Wentworth, 1996.

Bergmann, Barbara R. *Saving Our Children from Poverty: What the United States Can Learn from France.* Ithaca, N.Y.: Russell Sage Foundation, 1996.

Brown, Patricia. *Strategies for Linking School Finance and Students' Opportunity to Learn.* Washington, D.C.: National Governors' Association, 1995.

Chambers, Jay, and Fowler, William J., Jr. *Public School Teacher Cost Differences Across the United States: Analysis/Methodology Report.* Washington, D.C.: U.S. Government Printing Office, 1995.

Flowers, Rebecca, ed. *School Technology Funding Directory: The K-12 Decision Maker's Guide to Federal and Private Funds, 1999-2000.* Bethesda, Md.: IAQ, 1998.

Fowler, William J., Jr., ed. *Developments in School Finance, 1996: Fiscal Proceedings from the Annual NCES State Data Conference, July 1996.* Washington, D.C.: U.S. Government Printing Office, 1997.

Hunter, Barbara M. *From Here to Technology: How to Fund Hardware, Software, and More.* Arlington, Va.: American Association of School Administrators, 1995.

Monk, David H., and Brent, Brian O. *Raising Money for Education: A Guide to Property Tax.* Thousand Oaks, Calif.: Corwin, 1997.

Odden, Allan, and Busch, Carolyn. *Financing Schools for High Performance: Strategies for Improving the Use of Educational Resources.* San Francisco: Jossey-Bass, 1998.

Odden, Allan, and Kelley, Carolyn. *Paying Teachers for What They Know and Do: New and Smarter Compensation Strategies to Improve Schools.* Thousand Oaks, Calif.: Corwin, 1997.

Parrish, Thomas B., and Hikido, Christine S. *Inequalities in Public School District Revenues: Statistical Analysis Report.* Washington, D.C.: U.S. Department of Education, 1998.

Raden, Anthony. *Universal Prekindergarten in Georgia: A Case Study of Georgia's Lottery-Funded Pre-K Program.* Working Paper Series. New York: Foundation for Child Development, 1999.

Sherman, Arloc. *Poverty Matters: The Cost of Child Poverty in America.* Washington, D.C.: CDF Publications, 1997.

U.S. General Accounting Office. *School Finance: State Efforts to Reduce Funding Gaps Between Poor and Wealthy Districts. Report to Congressional Requesters.* Gaithersburg, Md., 1997.

Young, Beth Aronstamm, and Smith, Thomas M. *The Social Context of Education.* Findings from "The Condition of Education, 1997," No. 10. Washington, D.C.: U.S. Government Printing Office, 1997.

Chapter 8: Student Health and Education

Brown, Joel H., et al. *In Their Own Voices: Students and Educators Evaluate California School-Based Drug, Alcohol, and Tobacco Education (DATE) Programs.* Bethesda, Md.: Pacific Institute for Research and Evaluation, 1995.

Emihovich, Catherine, and Herrington, Carolyn D. *Sex, Kids, and Politics: Health Services in Schools.* New York: Teachers College Press, 1997.

Kronenfeld, Jennie Jacobs. *Schools and the Health of Children: Protecting Our Future*. Thousand Oaks, Calif.: Sage, 2000.

Pena, Robert A. *Principals, School Nurses and Other Health Care Providers: An Introduction*. 1998. ERIC No. ED424620.

Promoting Health Through Schools: Report of a WHO Expert Committee on Comprehensive School Health Education and Promotion. WHO Technical Report No. 870. Geneva, Switzerland: World Health Organization, 1997.

Chapter 9: Lifelong Learning

Cotton, Kathleen. *Education for Lifelong Learning: Literature Synthesis*. Research You Can Use: Lifelong Learning Series, Booklet 5. Portland, Ore.: Northwest Regional Educational Laboratory, 1998.

Hatton, Michael J., ed. *Lifelong Learning: Policies, Practices, and Programs*. Toronto: School of Media Studies, Humber College, 1997.

Holford, John; Jarvis, Peter; and Griffin, Colin, eds. *International Perspectives on Lifelong Learning*. Sterling, Va.: Stylus, 1998.

Longworth, Norman, and Davies, W. Keith. *Lifelong Learning: New Vision, New Implications, New Roles for People, Organizations, Nations and Communities in the 21st Century*. London: Kogan Page, 1996.

Longworth, Norman. *Making Lifelong Learning Work: Learning Cities for a Learning Century*. Sterling, Va.: Stylus, 1999.

Maehl, William H. *Lifelong Learning at Its Best: Innovative Practices in Adult Credit Programs*. San Francisco: Jossey-Bass, 2000.

Locating Current Information

One of the benefits of the Internet is the ability to obtain, in a matter of seconds, current information concerning topics of interest. Although the information in this book may become dated, the reader can access the latest facts about a subject by accessing the websites listed below. For example, many of the reports listed in this work are updated each year and posted on the Internet.

Educational Resources Information Center (ERIC) Database: http://ericir.syr.edu

As described on its website, "The ERIC database, the world's largest source of education information, contains more than one million abstracts of documents and journal articles on education research and practice. By searching AskERIC's web-based version of the ERIC Database, you can access the ERIC abstracts which are also found in the printed medium, *Resources in Education* and *Current Index to Journals in Education*. The database is updated monthly, ensuring that the information you receive is timely and accurate." The major method to find a document is to search using the keyword feature of the site's search engine. All searches may be limited by year of publication or publication type.

WALDO MetaSearch: http://waldo.rtec.org

This site is similar to the ERIC database, except that it searches for documents from all the following sites: the Eisenhower National Clearinghouse for Mathematics and Science Education, the Explorer Database (University of Kansas UNITE Group), the Educational Resources Information Center (ERIC) Database, and the Cross-Site Indexing Project (U.S. Department of Education).

U.S. Department of Education: http://www.ed.gov

Although the Cross-Site Indexing Project includes the U.S. Department of Education, users may limit their search to this site by using this site's search engine or by browsing the site's already prepared list of topics. There is also a list of the most requested items and the latest education headlines.

Amazon.com: http://www.amazon.com

To find books concerning education topics, access Amazon.com and execute a topic search using the site's search engine and limit the search to books. A list of books in and out of print will be generated. A similar online bookstore is BarnesandNoble.com at www.bn.com.

Yahoo.com: http://www.yahoo.com

Information posted on the Internet about a topic may be found using any one of the World Wide Web search engines. Just access the search engine, type the topic in the "search" area, and a list of sites will be generated. At the bottom of the page of Yahoo's generated list of sites, there are links to other search engines. When using a search engine that obtains documents from all sites on the World Wide Web, be certain of the source and verify the accuracy of the information. Remember that anyone can post information or misinformation on the Internet, and it is the user's responsibility to determine what is accurate.

Firstgov.gov: http://www.firstgov.gov

This site consolidates the government's 20,000 websites into a single location offering information about just about anything an educator can imagine.

About the Author

Dan H. Wishnietsky is an associate professor of mathematics at Winston-Salem State University in North Carolina. He holds B.S. and M.S. degrees in engineering from the University of California-Los Angeles and an Ed.D. in educational administration from the University of North Carolina at Greensboro. He also has minors in psychology and sociology.

Wishnietsky began his teaching career as a high school mathematics teacher and two years later started teaching mathematics at the community college level. He has taught at the university level for more than 15 years. His research interests are varied, and he has published works about sexual harassment, coaching, technology, mathematics, and learning communities. Wishnietsky also is a private pilot and has traveled extensively.

In all of his research and travels, Wishnietsky's goal has been to discover ways to teach that will help his students succeed in their education and in their lives.